*What Christians Can Learn
from Buddhism*

FACETS

Selected Titles in the Facets Series

What Christians Can Learn from Buddhism

Rethinking Salvation

Kristin Johnston Largen

Fortress Press
Minneapolis

WHAT CHRISTIANS CAN LEARN FROM BUDDHISM
Rethinking Salvation

Scripture quotations from the New Revised Standard Version of the
Bible are copyright © 1989 by the Division of Christian Education of
the National Council of Churches of Christ in the United States of
America and are used by permission.

Cover image: iStockphoto / red-frog.it
Cover design: Christy Barker

Library of Congress Cataloging-in-Publication data
Largen, Kristin Johnston, 1968-
  What Christians can learn from Buddhism: rethinking salvation /
Kristin Johnston Largen.
    p. cm. — (Facets)
  Includes bibliographical references.
  ISBN 978-0-8006-6328-5 (alk. paper)
  1. Christianity and other religions—Buddhism. 2. Buddhism—
Relations—Christianity. 3. Salvation. 4. Buddhism—Doctrines. I.
Title.
  BR128.B8L37 2009
  261.2'43—dc22   2008053701
The paper used in this publication meets the minimum require-
ments for American National Standard for Information Sciences—
Permanence of Paper for Printed Library Materials, ANSI Z329.48–
1984.

Manufactured in the U.S.A.

Contents

Acknowledgments

First and foremost, I would like to thank Richard Payne for his thorough reading of this manuscript and for his insights and suggestions, particularly in the Buddhism chapters. While I take full responsibility for any and all errors, the book is appreciably better for his attention and wisdom.

I would also like to thank my friends and colleagues on the faculty at the Lutheran Theological Seminary at Gettysburg for creating such a warm, vibrant academic community in which I work and thrive.

Finally, I would like to thank my husband, John, for his encouragement and support, not only in this project in particular but in all things.

Preface

At its core, I believe, dialogue between religious traditions is not just learning about another religion but also expanding one's understanding of one's own faith. With this in mind, the goal of this book is to introduce and describe the activity of interreligious dialogue: to explain why it is an important part of Christian faith development, and to give an example of what such theological activity looks like in practice. I write from the perspective that interreligious dialogue is a discipline internal to Christian systematic theology, and integral to the development and growth of Christian faith for all believers, rather than an external add-on for professional theologians only. Thus, I present interreligious dialogue not simply as an intellectual exercise for scholars only but as an experience of transformation for all Christians.

Interreligious Dialogue and the Christian Faith

With this book, then, I offer both lay Christians and those preparing for and engaged in professional ministry, as well as those in academia, the opportunity to explore how interreligious dialogue can deepen their own faith, using the example of the Christian doctrine of salvation. Specifically, I reexamine a Christian doctrine of salvation in light of an encounter with Buddhism, which I will introduce through the lens of the great Mahayana

Buddhist philosopher Nagarjuna and his teaching of emptiness, *sunyata*.*

While many resources are available for Christians to learn the basics of other religions, including Buddhism, fewer resources exist in interreligious dialogue that are geared to beginners and encourage them to reflect on the transformation of their own faith in the process of the dialogue. Yet many Christians with widely divergent backgrounds and differing levels of education are eager to learn more about how interreligious dialogue functions and how it affects the core beliefs of their own faith. Simply put, I believe that in the twenty-first-century world in which we live, this activity is essential for a vibrant, dynamic Christian faith; and I believe all Christians should be able to engage in it.

A Focus on Salvation

I have chosen the topic of salvation for several reasons, but, first, a word about terminology. I recognize that there will be those who object that the terms *soteriology* (a theological definition and explication of salvation) and *salvation* have such strong Christian connotations that it is inappropriate to apply them more broadly. However, while I agree that both words are typically associated with Christianity, this does not preclude their wider use. In fact, I would go further. I argue that it is necessary to see the goal of "salvation" as

---

*I have chosen not to use diacritical marks in the spelling of the technical terms that come out of Asian languages, such as Sanskrit and Japanese. As this book is intended as an introduction for beginners, such marks would be both meaningless and confusing.

the backdrop for most theological reflection in both Christianity and Buddhism. The primary reason for this is that both religious traditions offer descriptive and proscriptive means by which one might overcome the death and destruction that seem to characterize so much of human life.

Christianity describes a world of sin, forces of evil, and alienation from God, while Buddhism points to a world of suffering caused by delusions about personal identity and the cravings to which those delusions lead. Christians look to a divine savior for redemption and forgiveness, while Buddhists follow the Buddha's teachings to gain enlightenment. This brief contrast is, of course, too neat: many different practices and beliefs make up various forms of both Christianity and Buddhism, and thus there are many soteriological differences as well as some similarities. However, what is important here is the centrality of soteriological reflection in the overarching theological schemas of both traditions.

Orientation toward Salvation in Buddhism and Christianity

Both the Buddha and Jesus Christ state explicitly that the purpose of their teachings is for the salvation of the world, or at least of all sentient beings. Buddhism's soteriological emphasis is often given as the reason why the Buddha himself refused to engage in metaphysical speculation: anything that was not needed for liberation was unnecessary and a waste of time. The well-known example the Buddha gave was of the man who had been shot by an arrow. What was necessary to save the man was simply to remove the arrow, not to learn all the properties of the arrow or the cause for its flight. This emphasis on the liberation of others is also seen with particular clarity in the concept of the bodhisattva, who, out of compassion, takes a vow to forgo his or her own enlightenment until all beings have been liberated. In this way, the bodhisattva path is said to be consistent with the convictions of the Buddha himself, who also deferred his enlightenment to preach the Four Noble Truths and the Eightfold Path. Given the Buddha's own soteriological emphasis, it is fair to say that much of Buddhist theology assumes this central goal of enlightenment and liberation as its focus.

In a similar way, Jesus Christ stated over and over again, with various images and parables, his own soteriological purpose for coming into the world. He desired to make known God his Father, to proclaim the inbreaking of the kingdom of God, to forgive sins, to heal the sick, and to fulfill the Hebrew scriptures. Jesus gave his life in order to save the world; in so doing, he conquered sin and death, winning for humanity eternal life. For this reason, most, if not all, Christian teaching and preaching centers around both the understanding of what Jesus accomplished in his life, death, and resurrection and what ramifications his actions have for human life—whether it be defining our image of God, describing what it means to be human, or calling for a particular way of living in the world. This is why, in the Christian tradition, soteriology is one of the most comprehensive categories of theological reflection.

Both Buddhism and Christianity, then, in spite of the important distinctions characterizing them, share a similar soteriological orientation, even though the end for each is clearly different and the means by which the end is attained are dissimilar as well. These fundamental discrepancies must not be overlooked, and I cannot emphasize strongly enough that I am not trying to downplay or dismiss them. Rather, I am attempting to see them under the larger horizon of a much more cosmic vision of blessedness or deliverance. The *Oxford Dictionary of World Religions* defines salvation as "the act or state of being safe in ultimate terms."[1] This more inclusive concept of security, sanctuary, and peace is something to which all can relate, Buddhists and Christians alike.

Unfortunately, there is an almost irresistible pull for religious believers—particularly for Christians—to assume that their understanding of salvation is monolithic. After all, if a doctrine of salvation is to have the cosmic ramifications it claims to have, it seems to lose some of its heft and persuasion if its scope is limited in any way. Not surprisingly, this can create problems in interreligious conversations. This inherent, and often unconscious, bias that there is and can be only one true end or goal that encompasses all religions has hampered a full appreciation of other religious traditions and sometimes has created a false sense of unity where true differences actually remain. This stands in sharp contrast to a central aim of interreligious dialogue. In his book *Salvations*, Mark Heim writes, "What dialogue makes possible is for each tradition to develop the fullest and most rigorous and inclusive version possible of its distinctive convictions and life."[2] Too often we forget this in our eagerness to agree and in our zealous quest to find common ground. We thus cut off an avenue of dialogue that is rich with possibilities and insights.

New Ways of Understanding Salvation

Finally, on a more practical note, I believe that, for many Christians, issues of salvation very often are a central concern in discussions of non-Christian religions. This book will help Christians see a new way of thinking about salvation that moves beyond inclusive or exclusive categories. This perspective is particularly vital given that most popular writing on the topic of Christian salvation demonstrates a much more conservative view, insisting that salvation is necessarily limited to confessing Christians and leaving many believers to wonder about the future of their non-Christian friends, neighbors, and family members. My goal is that this book will help stimulate more creative reflection around this difficult and pressing question while still allowing Christians to hold on to their most treasured faith commitments.

In the end, I hope that the readers of this book will come away with the following: first, a new appreciation of the importance of interreligious dialogue for one's own faith enrichment and growth; second, a greater knowledge of the Buddhist religion; and third, a transformed understanding of the Christian doctrine of salvation.

1

The Task at Hand

What I attempt in the following chapters is a rethinking of the Christian doctrine of salvation through an engagement with Buddhism. Through this activity of interreligious dialogue, I hope to achieve a Christian theological end—that is, a Christian soteriological vision that both resonates with contemporary culture and also is enhanced by considered reflection on a non-Christian picture of the world.

I intend for my project to stand as both an example of a transformative, enriching interreligious dialogue and an illustration of the immeasurable value that this dialogue has for both constructing and interpreting key Christian doctrines. Christians, I argue, can learn things about themselves and their beliefs from other religious traditions that they cannot learn from their own. This makes interreligious dialogue an integral part of the task of any Christian theologian: in short, Christian theology *requires* consideration of and conversation with non-Christian religious traditions.

A word of authorial disclosure is warranted here. I want to be clear that I am writing as a Christian primarily for Christians, and that my intended audience is reflected in the nature of my approach and the direction of my argument. There are several reasons for this, not the least of which is my own background, education, and current institutional location. However, I would also argue that this type of dialogue cannot be done from a neutral standpoint: even if there were such a place—and, frankly, such a location is now and always has been a product of carefully constructed rhetoric and imagination—I would not choose to stand there. I speak as a Euro-American woman, a Lutheran pastor, and a professor at a Lutheran seminary; were I an African-American woman, a man from the Global South, a Muslim, or a Hindu, my reflections would be quite different. I do not pretend to speak from a purported universal standpoint to a purported universal audience; again, in the twenty-first century, such a claim is neither possible nor desirable.

What's more, interreligious dialogue functions best, I believe, when something is at stake—not when it is done from the safety of some presupposed position of academic detachment, with one's faith commitments carefully cordoned off. Interreligious dialogue benefits neither an individual believer nor one's broader faith community unless one's own beliefs are brought to the table and laid out. Only with this type of honesty and risk can transformation occur. Thus, while it is true that interreligious dialogue can have analogous benefits for members of other religions, and while I would suggest that the type of engagement I model here can and should be an integral part of religious discourse and formation for believers of all stripes, it is not my place to speak or work on behalf of other believers not in the Christian tradition. They must develop their own methodologies and shape their own dialogues. I would go so far as to say that the general pattern of this book can be applied broadly, but that the specific arguments and conclusions I draw are geared to Christians.

Can We? Should We?

Why should Christians engage in interreligious dialogue at all? Is there anything in the Christian tradition itself that would warrant, or even encourage, such an activity? It is a legitimate question and is not without answer. I suggest that there are two core Christian convictions that not only allow for but even promote conversation between religions: first, the nature of God as the creator of the cosmos; and second, the freedom of the Holy Spirit to blow where she will throughout the whole of creation.

The Nature of God

Christians have, from the beginnings of the tradition, understood God as the creator of the world, and this language of creation is a specific *interpretation* of the universe that makes very definite theological claims. *Creation* is not a neutral term—it is a declaration of faith. Traditionally, Christians have envisioned God's creative activity in two different ways. The first way that Christians describe God creating is *ex nihilo*, that is, "out of nothing." This doctrine emphasizes God's power over nothingness and annihilation: unlike all other creative agents, who need a material upon which to exercise their creativity, a substance out of which to construct something new, God, and only God, is able to call into being what is from what is not. Thus, this doctrine also emphasizes the uniqueness of the divine creative act: there is no other creative activity, certainly not in the human realm, that can compare to the divine act of origination.

The second formulation used to describe the creative activity of God is *creatio continua*, that is, "continuing creation." This doctrine emphasizes God's continuing relationship with the world, God's continuing involvement and providential care with creation. God has not simply created the world and then left it to its own devices. Instead, God is actively at work at every moment, in every aspect of the created order, nurturing and preserving it in love and grace. St. Augustine's famous formulation of this idea, used also by Martin Luther, is that creation is sustained only by the constant support of God's hand. If God were to withdraw that hand even for a moment, the whole of creation would fall into nothingness.

The other theological point affirmed in this doctrine is that day to day, year to year, God exercises the freedom to do "a new thing." Emphasizing the living, creative power of God reminds Christians that creation is not over and done with but continues anew every day. God's creative acts are not all in the past, moving further and further away from us as time passes. Instead, God's creative activity is present in the here and now and is even at work in the future, toward ends and goals as yet unforeseen and unimagined.

These claims about God's creative activity—that God has both created all things and continues to be in relationship to all things—reminds Christians that the entire cosmos, both as a whole and in each of its individual parts, is connected to God. And if this is true for all creation, it must be especially true for human beings, all of whom have been created in the image of God. Unlike other religions, Christians argue that whether people know it or not, or claim it or not, by virtue of God's universal creative activity, all people are linked to God. All people bear the fingerprints of being formed by God from the soil of the Garden of Eden; all people inhale and exhale the life-giving breath of God.

Therefore, from all of this, I argue that there are things Christians can learn about God from people who are, as I have said, connected to God but not in the Christian church. Just as any masterpiece bears the unmistakable mark of the master, so also all people, in all times and at all places, have the capacity to "bear" God and to witness in some way, in some form, to the one who created them. The way this works, of course, is a mystery; it is not something that Christians can prescribe beforehand or definitively identify. However, because of their belief in God, Christians can and should always be open to God's self-revelation, to seeing how God might be revealing Godself in the face of their neighbor, regardless of religious affiliation.

The Work of the Holy Spirit

The second theological justification for engaging in interreligious dialogue comes from a Christian understanding of the Holy Spirit. I take as my starting point here several descriptions of the work of the Holy Spirit in Scripture. John 3:8 reads, "The Spirit blows where it chooses, and you hear the sound of it, but you do not know where it comes from or where it goes." The symbol of wind or breath for the Holy Spirit emphasizes the life-giving power of God, as evidenced by the breath of God that vivified God's people in the dry bones prophecy of Ezekiel and the wind from God that drove back the Red Sea, allowing the Israelites to pass through on dry ground. But even more, it reminds Christians of the Spirit's dynamic freedom and vitality and the absolute inability of human beings to set a course for the Spirit or to predict where and when the Spirit will show up next. It warns Christians to resist stagnation and dogma-tism, and it demands that Christians stay open to the creative freedom of the Spirit to do the surpris-ing, the unexpected: the Spirit blows where she will, and it is impossible to know where she will manifest herself at any given time or place.

For this reason, too, Christians do not need to be afraid of the "inspiration" that may come in interreligious dialogue; rather, they are free to be open to the possibility that the Holy Spirit may well be at work in such conversation, guiding and shaping the work, filling those involved with wis-dom, grace, and peace. After all, the Holy Spirit is not a freelancer; the Holy Spirit was sent by Jesus, breathed into the presence of the disciples behind locked doors after the resurrection, and therefore we can trust the good intentions and the positive direction of her activity.

Interreligious Dialogue as an Act of Understanding

Having established a theological license for the dialogue, I imagine that for many Christians this proposal still seems very strange, even counter-intuitive, and may raise several questions: "Why would I, a Christian, need to engage in interreligious dialogue to learn something about my own God and my own faith? Isn't it enough just to study Scripture and the Christian tradition? Isn't it enough just to be in dialogue with other Christian believers?" Certainly, those activities are central to the development of one's faith, and I am not discounting them. However, I would argue that the depth and richness of one's faith development and, in particular, the level of understanding that one can achieve about God, the world, and humanity, are far greater when one makes the leap to engaging a religion different from one's own. In fact, this process of engagement has a very important connection to what it means to "understand" anything in the first place.

Any genuine act of understanding always has two components: the act of self-understanding and the act of understanding another. Human beings are fundamentally relational; therefore, as we learn about our world, we learn about ourselves at the same time, and vice versa. What this means is that learning something about someone or something else always generates a new way of understanding oneself at the time. This is why cross-cultural experiences frequently are so profound. It can be argued that we only really see and understand our own culture when we leave it and experience another culture different from our own. In the same way, as we grow in understanding of those closest to us—our partners, our children, our best friends—we begin to see ourselves differently and learn new things about our own emotions and actions.

What this means in interreligious dialogue is that every effort to understand the tradition or belief of one's conversation partner is always simultaneously an act of self-understanding, an act of reinterpretation of one's own faith and the relationship to the larger tradition in which one stands. I cannot emphasize enough that these two aspects of understanding cannot be sundered. If they are separated, the knowledge of another always remains at arm's length and never exercises transformative power on the understanding subject. In this situation, "knowledge of" never becomes "knowledge for," and one's understanding is never integrated into one's own life or reflected in one's own beliefs and actions. This, I would argue, is not true understanding at all. Therefore, I want to begin this particular example of interreligious dialogue by examining the relationship between these two aspects of understanding—understanding the self and understanding the other—and the ramifications this interpretation of understanding has for the work that lies ahead in the next chapters.

In thinking about these kinds of theological issues, I have found the work of Hans Georg Gadamer, a twentieth-century German philosopher, to be very helpful, especially the discussion in his magnum opus, *Truth and Method*. Gadamer's name is primarily associated with philosophical hermeneutics, and his work is primarily text-based; but his ideas have had important ramifications in other disciplines as well, including literary criticism and theology. Engagement with Gadamer's philosophy, then, has the potential to yield rich rewards in the discipline of interreligious dialogue.

Almost any interreligious dialogue involves remarkably diverse conversation partners who come from a wide variety of very different religious traditions. In these circumstances, the ability to genuinely understand one another is both critical and extremely challenging. It is critical because without that understanding, dialogue quickly becomes a monologue; it is challenging because the conversation, almost by necessity, deals with matters close to the heart for all parties. It is no easy task to see past one's own firm philosophical convictions and faith commitments into the worldview of another.

Thus, two primary temptations loom for those engaging in interreligious dialogue, even for those with the best of intentions: first, the desire to "convert" the other by showing the weaknesses in her tradition; and second, the willingness to jettison core commitments of one's own tradition in order to bolster claims of similitude. Both temptations must be avoided. I suggest that Gadamer's description of understanding (described below) is the best guide to help us navigate the conversation between Christianity and Buddhism, seeing us through to the goal of a richer, deeper vision of Christian salvation.

In the course of this specific argument, however, I hope to make the case for the broader position as well—that is, that Gadamer's concept of understanding is an excellent model for interreligious dialogue in general and that the principles he advocates can help those engaging in any form of interreligious conversation do two things better simultaneously. Even though Gadamer structures his argument primarily in terms of texts, his conclusions are equally appropriate to a dialogue between persons or traditions.

First, following Gadamer here helps individuals better understand their own traditions, strengthening their own articulation of their faith and bringing them fresh insights on familiar themes and arguments. In short, using Gadamer's concept of understanding in interreligious dialogue can help Christians become more conversant with and more appreciative of their own particulary beliefs and practices. Second, applying Gadamer's insights can help one genuinely appreciate and comprehend another's religious practices, reducing the chances of misinterpretation—or worse, exploitation and distortion. In what follows, then, I lay out several key aspects of Gadamer's description of understanding, which figure prominently in the activity of interreligious dialogue.

Understanding as Self-Understanding

The first aspect of Gadamer's thought that is relevant here is his notion that all understanding is self-understanding. Gadamer writes, "Someone who knows his way around a machine, who understands how to use it, or who knows a trade . . .

it still remains true that *all such understanding is ultimately self-understanding.*"[1] Often, we imagine the process of understanding as akin to observing something external to us through a microscope, identifying it, making note of its properties, and assigning it a classification. This process, we assume, does not change us in any way, does not ask anything of us, and remains firmly in our control at all times. This, says Gadamer, is not at all how understanding happens.

Rather, genuine understanding is always internal to us, rather than external. It includes a dimension of self-awareness and self-analysis, as it demands of us a reinterpretation of our own position in the world. Each time we understand something new, that knowledge changes us, to a greater or lesser degree, and thus each act of understanding requires that we see ourselves anew in relationship to the world. Each act of understanding creates new relationships and modifies old ones, in both subtle and grand ways, and thus over and over we must reposition ourselves in the world in light of who we become through each new act of understanding. If this were not the case, Christians would not be so uneasy about, for example, revelatory discoveries in science: from the Copernican revolution, through Darwin's theory of evolution, and up to and including cloning, all of these new ideas not only suggested a new way of understanding the world but also had radical implications for one's understanding of oneself. In the same way, albeit on a smaller scale, each book I read, each task I master, each friend I cultivate alters my worldview somewhat, even if ever so slightly. In understanding an occupation, a text, or another human being, my self-understanding is changed: by understanding the world in a new way, I understand myself in a new way as well.

What does this mean for this book? I argue that the challenge Gadamer raises here—or, rather, the reminder he offers—is that, as a Christian, I can never put aside or step out of my own faith commitments as I work in the field of interreligious dialogue. There is a way in which, at every moment, my own self-understanding is at risk because the possibility exists that I will come to such a radical new understanding of myself through the understanding of another text or another person that my former faith commitments will no longer satisfy me. The way I understand my relationship to God, the way I understand the economy of my own salvation—none of these views is immune to transformation or modification. Even the parts of myself I consider sacrosanct, such as certain core beliefs or fundamental convictions, are not above reinterpretation or even rejection, and I must be open to that possibility in order to allow for genuine understanding to take place. If I do not allow for the possibility of a new self-understanding, I automatically exclude the possibility of any true understanding of anything at all.

This is why risk and self-transformation are at the heart of any genuine interreligious dialogue. It is impossible to predict the direction in which the conversation will go or in what way I will come away from the table changed. All that can be said for sure is that in the very process of understanding another voice, another view, I will come to a fresh understanding of myself, my faith, my relationship to the church, and my relationship to God. This is inevitable, and I must be open to it.

Understanding as Event

Another important characteristic in Gadamer's notion of understanding is its event character. He writes, "All understanding is an event."[2] By that, Gadamer means that understanding is dynamic, not static, and that it changes over time and space. It is ever changing, ever evolving, and never occurs in the same way twice. The reason for this, of course, is that we are all different, and we bring to each event of understanding different histories and different backgrounds. A person, a text, or an idea speaks to each of us differently and challenges us in different ways. Thus, looking at Scripture, for example, not only do different individuals interpret the same passage of Scripture in vastly different ways, but also the same person interprets the same verses differently each time they are read. Particularly if a significant amount of time has passed between the first and second readings, the text will mean something different to the reader the second time around, and she will not see herself in the same relationship to the text as she did before. The way that Gadamer explains this phenomena is through the description of tradition.

Gadamer writes, "Understanding is to be thought of less as a subjective act than as participating in an event of tradition."[3] What Gadamer is emphasizing here is that no individual stands independently before a text or an idea and engages in the act of understanding autonomously. Instead, she comes before the text bearing the weight of her history behind her. Her religious tradition, her cultural tradition, and her socioeconomic tradition all shape the way in which she interprets the text or the conversation, and this, in turn, shapes those traditions as well. So, for example, each event of interreligious dialogue involving Christianity changes the Christian tradition, no matter how slightly, causing it to develop along different lines. This, in turn, affects the individuals within that tradition and modifies their future acts of understanding. In this way, an event of understanding is always an event of tradition, in which individuals participate. Understanding always occurs in the context of a larger community, never apart from it.

The conclusion Gadamer draws from this is that every event of understanding is inherently a creative event. He argues, "Inasmuch as the tradition is newly expressed in language, something comes into being that had not existed before and that exists from now on."[4] There is a genuine newness in understanding, a uniqueness that comes from seeing oneself and another with fresh eyes. In the course of the conversation, no one leaves the table unchanged; what's more, this change extends beyond the individual herself and affects the tradition as a whole. As Gadamer says, the language one uses to express one's own understanding is taken up and incorporated into the tradition, so that the tradition itself is renewed and modified. Our identities are not self-contained, and therefore what happens to us influences the whole context in which we live. The understanding of one individual stretches out far beyond the confines of her particular life, encompassing and affecting the whole tradition in which she stands. It is something like painting one wall of a room in a house. The new look changes not just that one wall but the appearance of the entire room, and sometimes even the entire house.

Understanding as Use

This dynamic character of understanding leads to the next characteristic of Gadamer's notion of understanding: understanding as use. Gadamer argues: "This implies that the text, whether law or gospel, if it is to be understood properly—i.e., according to the claim it makes—must be understood at every moment, in every concrete situation, in a new and different way. Understanding here is always application."[5] This emphasis on the need for a contextual, contemporary application of understanding is extremely important. What Gadamer is pointing out here is that every genuine act of understanding must include some incorporation into one's present situation—that is, there can be no understanding that is purely abstract, conceptual, and detached from one's here and now existence. To be genuine, understanding must be embodied—it must be lived. This means that the "I" who is engaging in the act of understanding cannot be forgotten, since, as Gadamer says, the text (or the interlocutor) makes a claim on her. That claim confronts her where she is and demands that she take notice. This, then, requires that she bring the new event of understanding into harmony with her current situation and apply it to her life now. Without this final act of reconciliation, the understanding always remains external, aloof, and ultimately impotent.

This does not mean that the original context is of no importance in interpretation. What Gadamer is advocating does not translate into plucking an idea or a theme out of its original context and plopping it down unreflectively in the present. This sort of irresponsible, egocentric

borrowing cannot ever pass for genuine understanding. Understanding as application always
presupposes the understanding of the text or, in
this case, the understanding of the other in her
own context. It is impossible to apply something
to one's own life without first entering into the
unfamiliar context and understanding it there,
on its own terms. Gadamer emphasizes:

> No one can stage a play, read a poem, or perform
> a piece of music without understanding the origi-
> nal meaning of the text and presenting it in his
> reproduction and interpretation. But, similarly,
> no one will be able to make a performative inter-
> pretation without taking account of that other
> normative element—the stylistic values of one's
> own day—which, whenever a text is brought to
> sensory appearance, sets limits to the demand for
> a stylistically correct reproduction.[6]

Thus, there are two very important steps that
are necessary for genuine understanding to occur.
First, each dialogue partner must understand the
position of the other in her own context, insofar as
it is possible. This requires intense listening, reading, and researching, all the while withholding
judgment, allowing the text or the person to speak
for itself or herself.

Only when this task has been satisfactorily completed can the next phase of understanding begin—
that is, the understanding that occurs through
applying the new knowledge to one's own context.
In this step, two things happen. First, the knowledge
is brought into the horizon of one's own tradition
and is brought to bear on the present circumstances—

that is, it is integrated into the values and norms of the here and now. This process of application is in itself understanding. This leads naturally to a deeper sense of self-understanding as well, as one sees oneself and one's own tradition differently in light of the new application of fresh knowledge.

Thus, in the work that follows, two things are required. First, the Christian reader must listen patiently and honestly to what Buddhism has to say about the world and about humanity. Buddhism must be allowed to speak its truth. Following that, the Christian must be able to take what he has learned and apply it to the insights of his own tradition, rethinking his own truth claims. Without either of these steps, understanding is truncated, either because the other has not been fairly heard or interpreted or because what has been learned is left at the table instead of being brought home. For interreligious dialogue to be effective and transformative, the knowledge gained must be applied; otherwise, there can be no genuine understanding or engagement.

Understanding as Understanding "Something"

The last aspect of Gadamer's description of understanding that I want to highlight is his insistence that all understanding is an understanding of "something." Gadamer's point is that those engaged in the task of understanding do not simply assert their will onto a blank slate, as it were. The object of understanding—for Gadamer, a text of some sort—has its own integrity and possesses its own truth. Therefore, the object of understanding is not just passive: it does not just sit there mutely waiting to be discovered. Rather, it speaks. In fact, it asks a question of its interpreter and turns the tables on the inquisitor by making him the object of inquisition. Thus, Gadamer says, "understanding begins . . . when something addresses us."[7]

This point is extremely important for interreligious dialogue. Neither the texts of another tradition nor the faith tradition of another believer can be railroaded to say anything that suits the purposes of the interpreter. For example, I cannot simply decide on some particular point or concept I want the Bible to affirm and then root around in Scripture until I find it. Nor can I tune out everything my Buddhist dialogue partner says with the exception of the parts that I like or those points that fit with my personal interpretation of God and the world. Such intellectual coercion denies both the text and the person their own sincerity and cohesion. Rather, the interpreter must abandon herself to the "other" as it is, not as she would like it to be, and allow herself to be challenged by what she finds there. In this way, she herself becomes the question, as she is forced to look at her own preconceptions in light of what the other is saying. Thus, Gadamer writes, "self-understanding always occurs through understanding something other than the self, and includes the unity and integrity of the other."[8] If the interpreter does not make a genuine attempt to understand something—a text, a person—outside herself, she will never move outside the walls of her own conceptions, and, as Gadamer emphasizes, she will never understand even herself truly, let alone another.

In the case of interreligious dialogue, then, Gadamer's point here reminds us that the conversation partner—be it a religious text, an individual, or the general study of a religion other than one's own—must be given genuine attention. This is often difficult, given that we all enter conversation with ideas we want to preserve and hypotheses we want to prove. It is very tempting to push forward our own agendas with stopped ears, giving the other only a cursory hearing on the way to confidently stating the conclusions with which we started. However, if we short-circuit the process of genuine dialogue this way, not only will we fail to ever understand anyone else's position but we will also never fully understand ourselves. This is why Gadamer argues that "conversation is a process of coming to an understanding."[9] It is this process that I am aiming for in the following analysis. Following Gadamer, then, my primary methodological commitment is a commitment to the dual aspects of understanding—that is, self-understanding and the understanding of another—that occur in the activity of interreligious dialogue.

Why Salvation?

From these methodological reflections I now want to turn to the specific subject matter of this project: the Christian doctrine of salvation. In the section that follows, I explain why I have chosen this particular theological category as the focus of this specific dialogue.

Soteriology is one of the most fundamental and foundational categories in Christian theology for two reasons. First, the scope of soteriological reflection is one of the most comprehensive of all theological topics or *loci*. In theological discourse, soteriology touches questions of anthropology,

Christology, and ontology, and it flows directly from consideration of both the nature of God and the nature of the God–human relationship. It is impossible to make compelling soteriological claims without including a discussion of humanity and what it is in us that needs redeeming, destroying, or perfecting. It is also impossible to discuss the saving work of Christ without including a discussion of his person as well. Finally, to ground a soteriology in a particular context, an appropriate worldview must also be articulated in order to harmonize what is promised or what is to come with what is now.

Even this is not all. Along with these individual categories, the relationship among them also cannot be ignored. Not only God but also God's relationship to the world and humanity must be taken into account. Is God a terrible judge, standing over creation waiting to pass sentence? Is God a loving mother, embracing creation in her arms? Or is God a mystery, unknown and uninvolved in the world's daily travails? The way salvation is defined in Christian theology is intimately linked with the way the world is described, the way God acts in relationship to the world, and the way human life unfolds in the context of the world. In short, Christian soteriology is integrally related to one's understanding of oneself, the world in which one lives, the God one worships, and the savior one needs.

Therefore, focusing this particular dialogue on the Christian doctrine of salvation opens up an unusually wide variety of conversations and questions and also has the potential to transform one's understanding in an exceptionally broad range of religious categories. There are many different points at which one can engage, and many different ways one's understanding can deepen and grow.

The Journey Ahead

To conclude this chapter, I offer a brief outline of how the following chapters unfold. In chapter 2, I introduce a Christian doctrine of salvation, including some of the central components that characterize it. This chapter will give the reader a solid beginning, a clear sense of what I mean, exactly, when I say "salvation," so that the reader has something specific to keep in mind when Buddhism is introduced and something identifiable to compare to new Buddhist concepts.

In chapter 3, I offer a brief introduction to Buddhism. This chapter contains two main sections: first, a general introduction to the basic concepts of Buddhism, including the life of the Buddha and the Buddha's central teachings; and second, a development of Buddhism over time and space.

In chapter 4, I first introduce the reader to the concept of *nirvana*—what it is and how one attains it. My lens for this discussion will be the Buddhist concepts of emptiness and dependent origination, specifically as they are described by the Mahayana Buddhist philosopher Nagarjuna. Then I discuss specific practices of Buddhism that are geared toward realizing *nirvana*. In chapter 5, I lead the reader through the work of self-examination and transformation. Now that the reader has been exposed to these critical concepts of Buddhism, we turn our attention back to the Christian doctrine of salvation and reexamine it with new eyes. This is the point at which the door is opened to a genuinely new understanding of one's own faith commitments. To facilitate this process, in this chapter I offer some points of discussion—traditional Christian concepts that are challenged or reenvisioned when viewed through the lens of the Buddhist doctrine of emptiness. For me, this is the payoff of all that has come before; this is the chapter where the reader puts it all together and takes the leap into the realm of transformation. I conclude with some thoughts about the endeavor of interreligious dialogue, and I reemphasize its importance for Christian faith in the twenty-first century. I encourage the reader to continue this enterprise, and I offer suggestions for how to proceed further, including a list for further reading.

2

A Christian View of Salvation

I n this chapter, I define and discuss a Christian doctrine of salvation that will serve as a
foundation for the dialogue with Buddhism that
is to follow. This approach is logical: to consider how an understanding and appreciation
of Buddhist doctrine might positively affect a
Christian articulation of salvation, we must first
establish parameters to define salvation in the
Christian tradition. However, this task is not as
straightforward as it might appear. Unlike the
doctrine of the Trinity and the doctrine of the
two natures of Christ, definitively set at the
Councils of Nicaea (325), Constantinople (381),
and Chalcedon (451), no definitive doctrine has
been established by the Christian church that
mandates one specific model or explanation of
how it is that Jesus saves. Both the New Testament and the writings of the early church fathers
contain a wide variety of explications of the
means through which Jesus brings about reconciliation, restoration, and new life. These different explications typically are called theories of
atonement, that is, doctrines that elaborate on
how it is that Jesus' life, death, and resurrection
constitute human salvation.

While this multiplicity of views might at first seem to be a disadvantage, I would argue that this plurality has great value. In the same way that having four Gospels instead of just one gives Christians a much richer, multifaceted picture of Jesus' life, death, and resurrection, so too having a variety of atonement theories gives Christians a wide range of language and images from which to draw when explaining the reality of God's saving grace and love in the concrete reality of human life in the world today. Having a wealth of resources at one's disposal allows one to communicate more effectively this essential truth of the Christian faith to individuals in a wide range of circumstances, thereby honoring the various ways the resurrected Christ is experienced by people today through the power of the Holy Spirit.

Given this multiplicity, then, it would be neither honest nor advisable to choose and endorse a single atonement model proscriptively. Instead, I take a descriptive approach, seeking to highlight characteristics that are important and relevant for shaping any twenty-first-century articulation of salvation. To do this, I have broken up this chapter into three main parts. In the first part, I begin with an anthropological/cosmological question: looking at the world today, what are the aspects of human existence that any doctrine of salvation must address in order to claim relevance and fidelity both to the Word and to the world? In answer to this question, I lift up three themes that dominate: sensitivity to cultural context, awareness of the environmental crisis, and the global cry for justice. This has the following ramifications for Christian soteriology: first, salvation must come in a recognizable, culturally suitable form; second, it must speak to the cosmos as a whole; and third, it must ensure that good triumphs over evil and that right is restored.

In the second part of this chapter, I briefly define and discuss the three motifs of atonement that have dominated Christian reflection on this topic through the centuries, particularly in the Western Christian church. Standing alone, each of these theories has serious shortcomings, but when viewed in conjunction with one another, each highlights one important component of the saving work of Jesus Christ. In the final part of the chapter, I enumerate five different tensions inherent in all explanations of Jesus' saving work, which must be maintained in any responsible discussion of salvation.

Salvation in Context

One important insight highlighted in the work of many liberation theologians is the need to make explicit the connection between theology and context. For example, Latina theologian María Pilar Aquino argues that in the postmodern world in which we live, we must face the reality that no single theology can offer us a "God's-eye view" of the world. Rather, we all are bound to our own "land's-eye views," which are conditioned by our nationality, socioeconomic status, race, gender, and so forth.[1] What this means is that all theology is perspectival; all theology reflects the circumstances in which it was developed, and it bears the stamp of a specific time and place. This does not mean that Augustine, for example, writing in fifth-century Africa, has no relevance for Americans in a twenty-first-century context, but it does mean that his understanding and articulation of theological truth was shaped by the specific concerns that dominated his context. Therefore, we cannot transport his insights uncritically into the present day without first analyzing how they were shaped by circumstances very different from our own.

As another example, Lutherans today need only take a cursory glance at Martin Luther's acerbic writings on the Jews to realize that not everything written by even the most honored theologians in one's tradition can or should be endorsed today. All theology—including all doctrines of God, all explanations of Jesus' person and work, all images of the church—is developed out of particular situations and speaks to particular groups of people. This is why theology is always changing, why there is always something new to say theologically in response to the new situations in which humans find themselves before God.

This has direct ramifications for a twenty-first-century doctrine of soteriology. This "doctrine-context" relationship, inherent in all theological reasoning, demands that any explication of how Jesus saves must be directly and intentionally related to the context in which it is articulated— that is, it must consider the historical context of the people to which it speaks. This requirement stands even though soteriological claims are, by their very nature, universal in scope: when Christians seek to describe God's saving work in Jesus Christ, they are not speaking about how God saves this group of people or that group of people.

Instead, a Christian doctrine of salvation attests to God's universal saving love and to the cosmic span of God's redemptive activity. Nonetheless, the way in which those claims are articulated at any given time must be context-sensitive and faithful to one's specific location. Otherwise, the message of salvation will have no resonance with people's lives and will be, in the end, incomprehensible and meaningless.

Salvation of the Cosmos

I now turn to the second characteristic required in a twenty-first-century soteriology: the incorporation of the physical cosmos into a holistic vision of salvation. Many theologians today would agree that it is irresponsible to make soteriological claims without including in one's analysis the grave environmental crisis facing our planet. Creation in and of itself—the physical world and our physical bodies—has been created and called good by God; therefore, creation itself has intrinsic value and must be included in a doctrine of salvation.

While this certainly is being stressed by theologians in a new way today, the idea itself is not new: the inclusion of the cosmos in soteriology has a long history in Christian theology, dating all the way back to Scripture and to the disciples' understanding of Jesus' ministry. The Bible interprets Jesus' ministry in cosmic terms, affirming that he came to save the entire universe, not just humanity. Thus, we read in John 3:16 that it was God's love for the entire cosmos that motivated God's sending of the Son, not God's love for humanity exclusively. In Colossians, we read that in Jesus, God was pleased to reconcile to Godself all things, both in heaven and on earth. Further, in Romans, Paul writes that the entire creation is groaning, waiting for the day when it, too, will be set free from its bondage to decay and will be given the freedom of new life. All these ideas come together in the "new creation" imagery of the New Testament, which proclaims that in Christ there is a new creation; and in the book of Revelation, which promises that this new creation will be realized when Christ comes again.[2] All of this is to say that Christian theology, from its inception, has argued that the salvation of humanity has been intrinsically linked to the salvation of the world.

Unfortunately, this connection has not always been emphasized; and unfortunately, in many places in Christian history one can see a distinct lack of interest in the physical cosmos and even an outright rejection of the participation of the physical world in the economy of salvation. In the twenty-first century, however, many theologians are reviving this important aspect of Christian soteriology. To examine the connection between the salvation of humanity and the salvation of the cosmos, I want to look at one such theologian, Ivone Gebara.

In her book *Longing for Running Water*, Gebara outlines an anthropology that takes seriously our concrete, physical location in and our relationship with the earth. She makes much of our existence as "earthly creatures," creatures of the soil. This phrase can be taken two ways. First, according to the account in Genesis, we have been created from the earth, a fact Christians remember each Ash Wednesday as we receive the ashes upon our forehead and hear the words "Remember you are dust, and to dust you shall return." We have, then, a profound physical connection to the earth that penetrates to the heart of who we are as human beings. Gebara describes it this way: "We are creatures of the earth, of the soil—and we live out of this terrestrial relatedness and feel an urgent need to rebuild it, to stop harming our own body, to stop exploiting and destroying it."[3]

We are earthly creatures in another way also. We are born in a specific place, and we are raised breathing air filled with certain smells, surrounded by certain landscapes. For someone like me, born and reared in Colorado, the mountains are "home" in a way that the seashore never will be. For someone else, born and raised in North Dakota, for example, "home" may be the wide-open plains. For someone else, "home" may be the sun and the beach. We have a connection to concrete places, to specific "lands" where we feel connected and rooted, and we reveal our earthly nature through these physical connections. The word for this phenomenon is *autochthony*, and it plays an important role in the development of our self-understanding. Gebara describes her own relationship with the soil this way: "My initial relationship with the earth is not with Earth as a planet that is part of the solar system, but with the earth on which I took my first steps; on which I smelled my first smells, both pleasant and unpleasant; on which, in time, I took firmer steps; and on which I jumped, rolled, and shed tears."[4] We are thus "earthly creatures" not only in general but also in particular, in ways that vary according to our specific lived experiences. Undeniably, therefore, a responsible soteriology must include consideration of "the cosmos"—both broadly and narrowly defined.[5]

Salvation Means Justice

The last characteristic of a twenty-first-century soteriology I wish to highlight is the incorporation of concerns of justice in the here and now into any understanding of what it means to be saved. In other words, to be meaningful at any given time and place, soteriology must speak to a present-moment experience of bondage and injustice in a way that relates a vision of "what will be" to the experience of "what is" right now. In any particular vision of salvation, the sin and evil that are experienced now must be harmonized with the good and the beautiful that are promised in the future. If the language of salvation evinces no care for or attention to the concrete physical and psychological suffering people experience today, it is very possible that the whole concept of salvation will seem meaningless; and that the confidence that God is with us in our present struggles, working to bring about justice and peace, will be shattered. What good is "the feast to come" if my children are starving today? What does it matter that "one day" I will be with Jesus if Jesus is not with me now?

Over the past few decades, few theologians in the United States have made that argument as strongly and as passionately as James Cone. In his early work, *A Black Theology of Liberation,* Cone forcefully makes the case that no theology can properly call itself liberating or "salvific" without a commitment to the marginalized and oppressed in society—in particular, African Americans. While it is tempting to relativize Cone's argument here and localize it exclusively within the boundaries of black theology, such an action would be a mistake. What Cone is emphasizing is true for all theology: the liberative praxis of Jesus Christ and the love of God, which Christ proclaimed to the world, are not meant to be seen in the abstract. Rather, God's love is concrete, for flesh-and-blood human beings, and Jesus' proclamation of the kingdom of God links salvation with action and change now.[6] If soteriology does not directly address concerns of injustice and oppression, it is not worthy to be called salvation discourse, and this is true for all people, regardless of their skin color. Cone insists that the future and the present cannot be separated in soteriological reflection: "Heaven cannot mean accepting injustice of the present because we know we have a home over yonder. Home is where we have been placed *now*, and to believe in heaven is to refuse to accept hell on earth. This is one dimension of the future that cannot be sacrificed."[7]

In a recent article, "Strange Fruit: The Cross and the Lynching Tree," Cone makes the same point using different language. He writes, "The gospel is God's message of liberation in an unredeemed and tortured world."[8] It is for this reason that he juxtaposes the image of the cross with that of the lynching tree: to remind Christians that the cross redeems the lynching tree and gives those whose bodies were broken on it final meaning and redemption, and also that the lynching tree keeps the cross from becoming a sterile, empty symbol. Connecting the cross and the lynching tree dramatizes the fact that any vision of liberation or blessedness must address those places where God's love is most desperately needed, where God's righteousness is most desperately required, where "salvation" must mean something right now if it is to mean anything at all.

Thus far I have argued that any doctrine of salvation that seeks to explain the saving work enacted by Jesus Christ for present-day Christians must include the following components: recognition of the relationship between doctrine and context, inclusion of the physical cosmos, and direct relevance to one's here-and-now experience of suffering and sin. These three components ensure that any contemporary discussion of salvation is both relevant and meaningful to Christians today. However, these components do not, by themselves, constitute a soteriology. For that, important questions still must be answered that look specifically at Jesus' life and death, and relate the particulars of his ministry and his crucifixion to salvation. For example, a doctrine of soteriology must explain how it is that life is brought out of death—something that seems, at first glance, to be both impossible and absurd. It also must address how the life and death of one removed the sin of all. And finally, it must speak to what role, if any, the kind of life and ministry that Jesus embodied has to play in an understanding of salvation. These questions are the focus of the various motifs of atonement examined below.

If the previous section looked at salvation through the lens of human existence today, the following section looks at salvation through the lens of Jesus' own life and death, seeking to highlight the aspects of Jesus' person and work that are central to a contemporary understanding of how Jesus saves.

Three Motifs of Atonement

In the course of the past two thousand years of church history, a wide variety of doctrines have been articulated that seek to explain—both to insiders and to outsiders—how it is that the Christian church understands Christ's saving work in the world. This variety is a result of both different understandings of Christ's person and of the different contexts in which they were articulated—contexts shaped by different intellectual movements, economic forces, and sociocultural dynamics. It would require another volume entirely to trace them all; thus, this task lies outside the scope of this chapter.[9] However, this chapter will discuss three motifs of atonement in particular that have greatly influenced the development of soteriology in the Western church: the "Christus Victor" motif, the "satisfaction" motif, and the "moral influence" motif.[10] While none of these motifs alone encompasses the full range of meanings present in Christ's saving work, each one offers a specific idea that is important to incorporate into any twenty-first-century discussion of salvation. From the Christus Victor motif, we take the power of Christ to conquer the death-dealing powers of sin and evil, in whatever forms they are found. From the satisfaction motif, we take the recognition that salvation is always a free gift, impossible to accomplish on our own. And finally, from the moral influence motif, we take the transformation that occurs in the individual once he or she experiences the saving power of Jesus Christ.

Jesus as Victorious Champion

The Christus Victor image is one of the oldest and most influential descriptions of salvation—not only in the theology of the church fathers but also in the contemporary context. For this reason, this particular motif is also sometimes described as the "classic" view of atonement. In this description of salvation, the overriding theme is the victory God has won in the resurrection of Jesus over the powers of sin, death, and the devil. In *Christus Victor*, Gustaf Aulén's seminal study of soteriology, this model is described as follows: "Christ—Christus Victor—fights against and triumphs over the evil powers of the world, the 'tyrants' under which mankind [sic] is in bondage and suffering, and in Him God reconciles the world to Himself [sic]."[11]

As is perhaps obvious, this particular picture of atonement retains strong mythic elements: the setting is a cosmic battle between good and evil—between God and the devil—with humanity caught helpless in the middle. Thus, this motif is characterized by warrior imagery, battle metaphors, and a vivid, very literal image of Jesus as king and lord. Because of humanity's inability to participate in or affect the outcome of this cosmic battle, there is no question of humans contributing anything or offering anything to the work of salvation in this model. Clearly, explicitly, everything needed for salvation is done for humanity by God and God alone. This is one reason why Aulén also calls this model a "dramatic" view of atonement, in that "it represents the work of Atonement or reconciliation as from first to last a work of God Himself [sic], a *continuous* divine work."[12]

Another interesting aspect of this motif is its lack of emphasis on the individual human being. Instead, it focuses on the redemption of the cosmos as a whole, and the action of God's saving work is presented not as taking place discretely, in each human heart, but rather in the form of "a drama of a world's salvation."[13]

This cosmic drama has been described in various ways through the centuries. One popular form of this model uses "worm on the hook" imagery. In this image, first used by Gregory of Nyssa, Satan devours Jesus like a fish devours a worm, unaware of the "hook" inside, and so brings about his own undoing. The model is grounded in the idea that Satan has humans captive and therefore God must "ransom" them back. God offers Satan Jesus, and Satan cannot resist this tempting bait. Satan "swallows" (destroys) Jesus and, in so doing, overreaches his power—that is, he takes what does not belong to him. Jesus is not simply a very powerful human being; rather, he is God, over whom Satan has no control or power. In that action, then, Satan himself is destroyed.

Martin Luther also used this image to describe the saving work of Christ. For example, in his *Sermons on the Gospel of John*, chapter 1, Luther writes: "For the hook, which is the divinity of Christ, was concealed under the earthworm. The devil swallowed it with his jaws when Christ died and was buried. But it ripped his belly so that he could not retain it but has to disgorge it. . . . This affords us the greatest solace; for just as the devil could not hold Christ in death, so he cannot hold us who believe in Christ."[14] Notice all that Luther has packed into this metaphor. There is a battle between Christ and the devil, with all humanity at stake. Reminiscent of the Trojan horse, Christ allows himself to be taken into the enemy camp, in order to surprise his foe and to free all those who are captive. Although Christ's victory really occurs in his death, as that is the moment when the devil "bites," so to speak, it is in his resurrection and exaltation that Christians celebrate their freedom.

In contemporary theological discussions, several limitations of this motif have been noted. First, some Christians find the mythological language here problematic: they do not think of the world as a cosmic battleground, with the forces of evil personified in a war with God and the powers of good. Second, many Christians question the idea of the devil having "rights" over humanity that even God must recognize. Third, some Christians question the idea of God, who is truth and light personified, using deception and trickery to overcome evil. Finally, others reject the absolute passivity of humankind in the face of evil and resist the notion that humans can do nothing to combat the power of sin.

However, in spite of all these disadvantages, what makes this image of atonement still powerful today is that it emphasizes in no uncertain terms that God is stronger than all the forces of evil that swirl dangerously around us, in both structural and individual forms of oppression, abuse, violence, and exploitation. Even though the power of sin seems terribly strong in the world, even though children still suffer and die from the evil deeds of others, and even though human society is still pervasively and deeply marred by injustice and terror, these evil powers will not have the last word—death will not win. Instead, in Jesus Christ, life and life abundant has been won for the cosmos, and in God's time, it will come to fruition for all, even when all signs appear to the contrary. Whatever else it may mean, salvation carries with it the promise that God is stronger than all the forces of sin, death, and the devil that conspire to take our lives—however these forces manifest themselves in the world. The power of love, the power of life, the power of healing and wholeness—a Christian doctrine of salvation proclaims the sure hope that, ultimately, these powers will win out and will reign supreme, not only for humans individually but also for human society as a whole and for the whole cosmos. This proclamation and this hope are a central aspect of any doctrine of salvation expounded today.

Christus Victor for Today

Before leaving this particular understanding of salvation, it is worth noting a contemporary update of this motif that has been laid out by Dennis Weaver. He calls it "Narrative Christus Victor," and he emphasizes that it is a nonviolent theory of atonement. Weaver is particularly concerned about atonement models that depend on violence— one model that comes under particular critique by Weaver is Anselm's "satisfaction" motif, which will be discussed shortly. Weaver explicitly rejects any understanding of salvation that seems to support "the compatibility of violence and retribution with the gospel of Jesus Christ."[15]

Weaver has several important updates to the classic Christus Victor model. First is his understanding of Satan or the devil. For Weaver, the figure of the devil is "the accumulation of earthly structures that are not ruled by the reign of God. This devil is real, but it is not a personified being who may or may not have rights in the divine order of things."[16] This allows Weaver to acknowledge the very real power of evil in the world without establishing another divine/semidivine being who has some sort of bargaining rights with God.

Second, Weaver emphasizes that the drama played out between good and evil does not happen just at the cosmic realm but also takes place in the midst of human history and thus has very practical, tangible effects for human existence. To support this claim, Weaver argues that the book of Revelation and the four Gospels tell the same story—one from a cosmic perspective and the other from a human historical perspective. Thus, according to Weaver, in Revelation 5–7, what is celebrated is "the victory of the reign of God over the rule of evil that slaughtered the lamb, Christ."[17] He writes, "The symbolic imagery in the scene of the throne room and the celebration that culminates the opening of the seven seals presents an awe-inspiring and thrilling message, namely that the resurrection of Jesus Christ is the ultimate and definitive cosmic victory of the reign of God over the rule of Satan and the multiple evils that he produces, including war and devastation, pestilence, and natural disasters."[18]

For Weaver, this "slain lamb" is the nonviolent conqueror, the same nonviolent Jesus that we meet in the Gospels, and thus, unlike the classic Christus Victor model, here Jesus' life is equally as important as his death, as we see the victory of God over the powers of sin, death, and the devil enacted in Jesus' ministry on earth, not exclusively in the heavenly realm. What's more, Jesus' ministry shows us something new about how God wins God's victory—not by a greater show of violence and power but by nonviolent resistance to evil. Weaver gives the examples of Jesus "turning the other cheek" and "going the extra mile" as evidence that Jesus "was teaching nonviolent ways for oppressed people to take the initiative, to affirm their humanity, to expose and neutralize exploitative circumstances."[19] Thus, what we see in the Gospels is that Jesus himself embodies the reign of God and that his ministry shows what the reign of God looks like over and against the social order.

Finally, Weaver is very clear that the violence that crucified Jesus was the result of human evil and does not have its origin in God. Unlike the classic Christus Victor model, God does not offer up Jesus or sanction his death; Weaver is clear that God did not demand the death of Jesus—the death of Jesus was not needed to inaugurate the reign of God. Instead, Weaver argues that "Jesus' mission was not to die but to witness to the reign of God. Jesus died not via divinely instigated violence but at the hands of those who represented the powers opposed to the reign of God."[20] This motif has important ramifications for Weaver, who argues that this vision of salvation contains within it a key ethical component. In response to God's saving grace, Christians are called to follow Jesus and to live a new life, repenting of the evil we have committed against God and our neighbor. Thus, Weaver writes, "Narrative Christus Victor pictures humankind actively involved in history as sinners against the rule of God, and as actively involved in salvation as the transformed individual participates in witnessing to the presence of the reign of God in history."[21]

Weaver's model is an excellent example of why the "how" of salvation must be continually reinterpreted anew, and how any doctrine of salvation always reflects the cultural context out of which it was developed.

Jesus as Our Satisfaction

The "satisfaction" motif is one of the most well-known models of atonement, thanks to its greatest proponent, Anselm, and his famous book *Cur Deus Homo*. In this work, Anselm attempts a rational explanation for the incarnation—hence the title, which translates as "Why God Became Human." Given what already has been said about the importance of recognizing the role one's context plays in theology, it is worth noting here that one motivation for Anselm was his negative view of the Christus Victor image, as he rejected the idea that the devil has any "rights" over humanity. Other names for this motif include the "penal substitution" model, the "substitutionary" model, and the "blood atonement" model.

In this motif, the setting is not a cosmic drama with humanity as a mere spectator. Instead, humanity takes center stage; in fact, humans are the source of the whole rupture in the God-human-cosmos relationship. For Anselm, the problem is that humanity, in our sinfulness, has disrupted the cosmic order and violated both God's justice and God's will for a harmonious creation. However, although humanity caused the problem, humanity cannot fix it: it is not in humanity's power to pay restitution to God, because nothing of human origin possibly can compensate for a stain on the divine honor. In other words, original sin is an infinite offense against God and puts humanity in the position of owing an infinite debt to God. Humanity owes the debt, which humanity cannot pay, but while only "God" can compensate "God," God does not owe anything. It is a seemingly insolvable problem, but Anselm has a solution, which he elaborates in the form of an answer to the question he asks in the title of the book—again, "Why God Became Human."

Anselm's answer to the question of the incarnation is that in no other way could God have received "satisfaction" for the offense of human sinfulness and restored the right relationship between God and humanity. Only God could provide the necessary satisfaction, but only a human could offer that satisfaction on behalf of humanity—hence Jesus Christ, fully human and fully God. The medieval context of Anselm's model includes an ecclesial structure in which penance was demanded as a payment for sin, as well as a feudal system of lord and vassals where an oath bound the vassal to the lord and obligated service and loyalty on behalf of the former in return for a piece of land and protection. If the vassal broke that oath, he could be subject to serious penalties. In this context, a system like Anselm's becomes quite understandable. First, Anselm did not grant that God could simply forgive humans the offense of their sinfulness; instead, God had to be repaid somehow, otherwise, the offense would remain, defying God's justice, and this would constitute a permanent blot on God's good creation. Second, Anselm argued that God also could not simply have chosen eternal punishment for humanity, even though that punishment was justly deserved, because this would have thwarted God's grace and mercy as well as God's good intention for creation as a whole. Neither of these solutions was possible: for Anselm, to maintain cosmic order, to preserve divine justice, and also to fulfill God's will for creation, the stain had to be removed. Humanity had to be punished yet also somehow forgiven; hence the death of Jesus—fully divine and fully human—on the cross.

Not surprisingly, this motif also has been criticized on several grounds. First, the imagery here is extraordinarily legalistic and seems to imply some form of cosmic law to which even God must adhere. God is not free to do as God chooses but instead must obey certain rules of the game; and when humanity rebels against God, God finds Godself in a bind, so to speak. Even God is powerless against the metaphysical structure of creation, which demands justice.

Second, and in the twenty-first century even more importantly perhaps, this model makes God the author of the crucifixion, and a seemingly very bloodthirsty one at that. A sacrifice is required to sate God's desire for recompense—and not just any sacrifice, but the sacrifice of God's own Son. What kind of a God is it, many theologians ask today, who demands the death of God's own beloved as a blood price for the stain against God's honor? Is this not some sort of divine child abuse? And what, then, does this say about our own relationship with God? If this is the face of the God Christians call "Lord," then, like Ivan Karamazov, maybe we should rather return our ticket and opt out of the whole relationship altogether.

However, these trenchant criticisms notwith-standing, what Anselm's model does emphasize is the powerlessness of humanity to win salvation for ourselves. In a twenty-first-century context in which we are accustomed to believing that we can do it all and have it all—that we are limited only by the power of our imagination and the strength of our will—Anselm's model reminds us of a sober-ing truth: on our own, we cannot "right" our rela-tionship with God. No matter how hard we try, no matter how good we act, no matter how much we pray or read the Bible, we cannot on our own work ourselves up to God or earn God's favor. We are hopelessly mired in our sin, and no amount of human willpower can get us out. God's action is required for our salvation, and any responsible Christian talk of salvation must always keep this fact foremost in mind.

Jesus as Moral Influence

The last motif of atonement to be discussed here is the "moral influence" model, which tradition-ally has been associated with Peter Abelard. This model is sometimes called the subjective motif of atonement, which is what Gustav Aulen calls it in *Christus Victor*. Unfortunately, this description has led to an inaccurate caricature of Abelard's thought, such that salvation becomes something we do rather than something God does for us. However, while there are undercurrents of this idea in this motif, and while if it is pushed too far such a charge might stick, overall, this characterization is unfair. It certainly is true that Abelard empha-sizes the transformation that occurs in us—this is where it gets its "subjective" categorization—but

the motif does not begin and end with humanity alone. Abelard is very clear that salvation as a
whole, and this transformation in the individual in
particular, is not the work of the individual per se;
rather, it is God's work in us.

This is why the term *moral influence* can be a
bit misleading. It is true that, for Abelard, Jesus
provides a moral example for humanity, particularly through the grace and love he evidences in
his life and ministry. However, this is not all Jesus
does: Jesus is not simply another "good" human
being—another prophet, another saint, another
sage after whom we should pattern our lives to the
best of our ability. Instead, because of Jesus' divine
nature—he is God incarnate, after all—Jesus does
more than simply provide us an example that we
have to follow by our own power. Instead, because
of Jesus' divinity, the example of his life is itself
compelling and efficacious: Jesus' love works love
in us, so that our own love that grows in response
to God's love in Jesus is also a work and gift of
God. There is a persuasive power in God's love that
makes Jesus more than just an exemplar; Jesus is
not only the model for human love but the power
of that loving.

This image of atonement also was used by many
of the so-called Liberal Protestants, beginning
with Friedrich Schleiermacher, who also lifted up
Jesus as a moral example and emphasized what he
called Jesus' "God-consciousness." By this term,
Schleiermacher intended to indicate that, in Jesus
Christ, God comes to each individual and that the
salvation of each individual lies in the realization of one's own union with God. Jesus' "God-
consciousness" was perfect; therefore, those who

come into contact with him—through his body, the church—also participate in this perfect union with God. This depiction of salvation also emphasizes the subsequent acts of love and justice by each individual, made in response to the individual's prior experience of God's love.

The primary weakness of this motif has been noted above and is signaled in the other name often used to describe it: the subjective model of atonement. Critics argue that, in this view, salvation is less of an objective reality—true whether or not humans experience it or realize it, and more of a subjective reality—dependent on one's actualization of it. What if no visible transformation occurs in an individual? Does this mean that salvation hasn't happened to him or her? And further, what constitutes transformation? How does one determine that transformation has occurred? When this idea is pushed to its limit, it seems to make Jesus' work alone not enough, and it demands some sort of human response in order for salvation to actually take place.

However, even in light of those criticisms, it is important to note that this motif still upholds a key component of salvation: the conversion that occurs in each individual through the power of God's love and mercy. Either salvation makes a difference in one's life or it doesn't, and if the Christian church claims that it doesn't, it is hard to imagine what difference it really makes at all. Future promises that have no relationship to life in the world today are meaningless and can hardly be expected to nurture in anyone the desire for a life of discipleship and faith. The abstract knowledge that comes from someone telling a person that she is saved is quite a different reality from someone experiencing that knowledge in an intimate, personal way: it's like being told secondhand that someone loves you versus looking into someone's eyes as she tells you herself. Part of the reality of salvation in the Christian tradition is God's personal "I love you," told directly to each person, and this motif is a reminder of that.

Each of these motifs, then, offers an important insight into the heart of what salvation in Jesus Christ has meant in the Christian tradition. Christus Victor celebrates Jesus' victory of life over death, and the destruction of the power of evil; Anselm's satisfaction reminds us that our reconciliation with God and the forgiveness of sins is a free gift that we cannot earn and do not deserve; and finally, Abelard's moral influence points to the transformation in the life of a Christian once she or he experiences salvation in his or her own life. The picture of salvation is richer when all are held together.

Salvation Talk and Tensions

In this final section, I want to add one more piece—actually, five more pieces—to the mosaic of salvation that I have constructed in this chapter, this time from the perspective of the language and images Christians use when describing the experience of salvation and answering such questions as "What does salvation look like?" and "What difference does salvation make?" and "How does salvation happen?" This section points to the inherently dialectical character of all "salvation talk." In the same way that all Christian discussion of humanity must include the two poles of saint and sinner—that is, humanity as both inherently good and redeemed by God and also permanently, indelibly stained by sin and in rebellion against God—so also must all Christian discussion of salvation maintain the tension between the opposing poles of human experience and God's self-revelation in that experience. These tensions are visible both in Scripture and in the Christian tradition, and in all five cases, if either pole is lost, a key insight into a doctrine of salvation is also lost. There is no way to reconcile these poles; they simply must be held together.

Salvation "Now/Not-Yet"

The first tension points to the "when" question: When do we experience salvation? Is it only something for the afterlife, or does it have some visible manifestations in human lives right now? The answer to the latter portion of this question is yes: therefore salvation in Jesus Christ is necessarily both "now" and "not yet." First, the "now." Without the promise of experiencing salvation now, God's promises of new life, forgiveness, and healing have no relationship to the present and no meaning for people in their daily lives. Recall what was said earlier about salvation being relevant to people's lives today and speaking to them in the midst of their pain and suffering: if all Christians can say to people is, "Don't worry, you'll be in heaven with Jesus one day," they are missing out on a central aspect of the good news: the inbreaking of the kingdom of God that is happening in the world *right now*. Remember Jesus' words in Luke

4, when he stood up in the synagogue in Nazareth and read from the scroll of Isaiah: "The Spirit of the Lord is upon me, because he has anointed me to bring good news to the poor. He has sent me to proclaim release to the captives and recovery of sight to the blind, to let the oppressed go free, to proclaim the year of the Lord's favor. . . . *Today this scripture has been fulfilled in your hearing*" (emphasis added). In the Gospels, the signs of salvation are all around Jesus: the hemorrhaging woman is healed, the paralytic is made to walk, the man with the unclean spirit is brought back into the community, and sinners are welcomed to feast with Jesus. For these and for so many others who came in contact with Jesus in the course of his ministry, salvation was experienced right then, as they felt the power of Jesus' life-giving touch and received a new life from that day onward.

So it is also with God's people today. The power of God's grace, forgiveness, mercy, and healing makes a difference right now. Even if it is not always perceived, it is there working transformation in and around the lives of every one of God's children. Salvation is not simply some pie-in-the-sky dream, a fantasy that can only be imagined and not really experienced. Like Jesus himself, the reality of salvation can be seen, touched, and embraced, right in the midst of human existence, in all its complexity, yesterday, today, and tomorrow.

Yet this is only one pole of the dialectic. As we know all too well, these signs of the inbreaking of the kingdom of God are not the only signs that surround us. Even though Jesus Christ has come into the world, even though the final victory over death has been won, in this "in-between time," we still see the signs of the power of death, as war, violence, oppression, hunger, and abuse still are evident in the lives of each one of us. Christians do not now, nor will they ever in their lifetimes, experience the fullness of salvation here and now. Now there is only "a foretaste of the feast to come," a glimpse of what perfected human existence will look like in the kingdom of God. In the meantime, we must struggle against the manifestations of sin and evil in ourselves, in others, and in the structure of society as a whole: weeping has not yet changed to dancing; morning has not yet come.

It is in this context, then, that we can make sense of Jesus' farewell prayer to his disciples in the Gospel of John. As he is leaving them, Jesus tells his disciples many things, not the least of which is a warning that hard times are ahead. The world may hate them, he says; they may be persecuted; there will be sorrow; there will be grief; and the world will cry out in pain, just as a mother cries out when she is in labor. But one day, all the pain and anguish will be behind them, as they will again be with Jesus in joy. So, too, with God's people in the world today. Salvation is both "now" and "not yet," because Jesus has come and in his life and work we have seen a vision of the new creation. That new creation, however, is yet to be fully realized, and only God can bring it about: without the "not yet" of salvation, Christians run the risk of forgetting that the coming of God's kingdom is in God's time, not ours. The temptation is to put all their hopes on one specific political, ecclesial, or social system, which ultimately only results in disappointment and disillusionment when said system does not bring about the desired changes. Both the "now" and the "not yet" poles of salvation must be held in tension.

Salvation Both Individual and Communal

Another dialectic that must be maintained when describing the experience of salvation is the communal versus the individual aspects. In American society, the individual dominates. This is a holdover from the Enlightenment emphasis on the individual knower as the arbitrator of truth; and in this country we continue to view discrete individuals as primary, and the relationships they form as only secondary and not inherently constitutive of an individual's personhood. I have argued elsewhere that it is as though individuals were LEGOs that can be snapped together and then snapped apart without any constitutive change to the individual LEGO itself. With this view of reality, it is no wonder that the individual aspect of salvation has dominated: it is the foundation for a theology that makes one's personal decision for Jesus the key to one's salvation.

While I think this view of salvation has grave weaknesses and, in fact, does not accurately represent human existence, I want to acknowledge what it preserves about the experience of salvation—that is, its *pro me* characteristic. This is the phrase Martin Luther used to emphasize the fact that God loves *me*, died for *me*, saves *me*, and thus has initiated a personal, intimate relationship with *me*. If salvation is only on a communal basis, a blanket forgiveness that universally and impersonally covers all, we risk reducing each individual—who has

immeasurable worth and value before God—to ano-
nymity and insignificance. In this purely communal
view, where is the God who "has searched me and
known me," who "formed my inward parts," who
"knit me together in my mother's womb"? Where
is the God who counts the hairs on my head and
knows the movements of every sparrow? Salvation
is not merely a general phenomenon; it also has a
very particular, intimate character that cannot be
overlooked or ignored.

However, on the other side of the dialectic,
if salvation occurs only on an individual basis,
our communal, interpersonal reality seems to be
denied and violated. This is merely one of the grave
defects in the popular Left Behind series of novels,
which seems to endorse the view that the relationship each person has with God is exclusively
individual and does not take into account the way
in which we are shaped and formed—and indeed,
only realize our full humanity—in community: in
our families, with our friends, in our communities,
and in our churches. What kind of heaven will it
be if our loved ones are not with us; or, even more
horrible to imagine, if those in heaven actually
can see the suffering of their loved ones in hell?
It is hard to image the experience of eternal bliss
coexisting with the knowledge of the eternal suffering of others. Nor is it possible to image that, in
heaven, we will somehow forget our loved ones,
as though we were never in intimate, meaningful
relationships with them in the first place. If continuity is to be preserved between who we are now
and who we will be in the future, somehow those
relationships must be honored and transformed
along with each individual.

There is good warrant for this communal aspect of salvation in Scripture. Look, for example, at the actions of the resurrected Jesus. In both John's and Luke's accounts of the resurrection, we see how Jesus does not forget his disciples, and how the relationships they formed while he was on earth are still a part of his resurrected existence. He comes to them, speaks with them and eats with them; most poignantly, he allows Thomas the doubter to touch him, and he allows Peter to redeem his threefold denial with a threefold affirmation of his love and devotion to Jesus. Jesus has not forgotten his friends—nor will we. Those relationships that have been integral to our lives here and now, those people whose love and care have formed and shaped us, will not be forgotten or left behind. Instead, they will be a part of our resurrected lives, too, and they will share in the joy of new life with us.

Salvation Includes Both God's Work and Our Work

At the outset of a discussion of this particular dialectic, let me be clear: I am not trying to argue here for a form of works/righteousness in which we somehow cooperate with God in the accomplishing of our salvation. As a Lutheran, I appreciate the emphasis on salvation coming through God's grace alone—the work of Jesus Christ is the only work able to save us. As Paul writes in Romans, all have sinned, and all have fallen short of the grace of God; therefore, no one can boast in any work of his or her own regarding salvation—it is a full and free gift to each Christian equally.

What's more, if we lose the concept of salvation as God's work, what should be a cause for rejoicing becomes a horrible death sentence, like it was for Martin Luther before his theological breakthrough. What should be gospel—the gift of salvation—becomes just one more law we cannot live up to, leaving us constantly in doubt as to whether we have done enough, whether we believe enough, whether all our efforts will really be enough. The recognition of salvation as God's work alone preserves us from that.

However, there is a danger on the other side as well, one that Lutherans historically have not articulated very well. If we lose the connection between anything we do in our lives here and now and the promised future salvation, we run the risk of falling into two destructive patterns of behavior. On the one hand is the danger of quietism—that is, turning a blind eye to sin in the world and feeling no responsibility for the welfare and care of our brothers and sisters. If our works don't make a difference in our salvation, why bother? Let someone else shoulder the burden and take the risk—there's nothing in it for me; I already have my reward. In light of such indifference, it is no wonder that the writer of the book of James fumed that faith, by itself, without works, is dead. What good is one's faith if it rusts in neglect, buried like a talent in the ground? This is not what God intends in the gift of salvation.

On the other hand is the danger of antinomianism, which reasons that since God loves and forgives me no matter what, since my salvation is already assured, I might as well have some fun; and if that means hurting others or taking advantage of them, oh well—ultimately, it doesn't matter. Again, if we completely disconnect our actions in our lives here and now from the life to come, we can forget the call to discipleship, the command to follow Jesus and walk in his footsteps, the mandate to incarnate Christ in the world in our own words and deeds. The fact that salvation is a free gift does not alleviate our Christian responsibility for ethical, loving action in the world here and now; a joyful, grace-filled life in the world also is a part of what it means to be saved.

Salvation Speaks to Both Christians and Non-Christians

One of the most difficult questions when it comes to salvation is the status of non-Christians. More and more Christians today are wrestling with the issue of how a Christian understanding of salvation relates to faithful believers of other religious traditions. On the one hand, problems arise when salvation is limited to Christians only. What about good and righteous people who are not Christian but who lead lives any Christian would be proud to claim? Is there no place in heaven for Gandhi or the Dalai Lama? Don't their lives of peace and goodness reveal the presence of the Holy Spirit? If God is in relationship to the whole world by virtue of creating the whole world, and if God's Spirit truly blows where she will, how can Christians be sure that God is not at work in a salvific way in non-Christians, and even in non-Christian religions?

The documents from the Second Vatican Council certainly recognize such a possibility. *Nostra Aetate* says: "The Catholic Church rejects nothing of what is true and holy in these [non-Christian] religions. She has a high regard for the manner of life and conduct, the precepts and doctrines which, although differing in many ways from her own teaching, nevertheless often reflect a ray of that truth which enlightens all men [sic]."[22] And further, the document *Lumen Gentium* states that God is not remote from "those who in shadows and images seek the unknown God, since he [sic] gives to all men [sic] life and breath and all things."[23] Therefore, the document continues, "those, who, through no fault of their own do not know the Gospel of Christ or his Church, but who nevertheless seek God with a sincere heart, and, moved by grace, try in their actions to do his [sic] will as they know it through the dictates of their conscience—those too may achieve eternal salvation."[24] How is it possible, then, in today's world to articulate a model of salvation without including non-Christians?

But this is only one side of the dialectic. On the other side, Christians also must face the reality that the faithful believers of other religious traditions have their own unique teleologies—that is, they have ends and goals all their own, and they have no desire to be roped into heaven, so to speak. Christians, of course, believe that heaven—eternal, perfected life with God—is the highest end possible, and therefore they desire (or should desire!) that all people will achieve it. However, at the same time, it makes no sense to hope for heaven for a Buddhist, for example, when she is working toward the full realization of her Buddha nature and the enlightenment of all sentient beings. A "one-size-fits-all" soteriology that takes no note of religious differences somehow seems unfaithful to everyone, as it minimizes the religious choices and beliefs one has made in one's earthly life and imposes uncritically the same destiny on everyone. Salvation becomes an abstract concept with no relationship to people's concrete, daily lives. Somehow, a Christian doctrine of salvation must deal with the possibility of God's grace upon and presence with those outside the Christian church while still upholding the important soteriological differences that separate believers from one another.

The Power of God's Grace and the Power of Human Freedom

I want to end with this last tension, because, in some ways, it is the most difficult to maintain. First and foremost, it is clear from Scripture that God wills that *all* be saved: Christ came for all, Christ's death is efficacious for all, and God loves all. However, it is also clear that humans reject Jesus and do not believe in him, and Scripture warns us that those who do not believe will not be saved. The question becomes, then, how do we balance the "yes" of God with the "no" of humanity? What do we do with the tension between God's gracious invitation to new life and the sinful rejection of that gift through human free will?

Again, on the one hand, it is important to preserve human freedom; without it, we are not fully human but, rather, puppets who jump up when our strings are pulled and walk where we are led. The Christian tradition clearly has rejected such an anthropology, arguing that God chose to create humanity with free will, even though God was aware of the possible consequences. The risk was worth it because only adoration that is freely given is valuable, only honor that is freely rendered is meaningful. God wants to be in a truly loving relationship with humanity—not in the sort of relationship that a master has with his slave, who is forced to stay, forced to respect, and forced to obey him. Instead, God desires the type of relationship that a partner may have with his spouse or a mother may have with her child. Such a relationship requires genuine human freedom, and if, in the end, God drags everyone into heaven with or without his or her consent, such a relationship seems to be violated. Thus, the "no" of humanity somehow must be honored.

And yet, can one believe that our will is equal to God's? Certainly, God's "yes" must be stronger, greater, more compelling than any "no" with which humanity might respond. We might compare a father who offers his young daughter a bite of a new tasty dessert that she has not yet tried. She might first say no—she might even say no a few times—but if the father persists, eventually she may well give in, and after tasting the treat she will realize how foolish she was to refuse it. Sometimes humans say no to God out of ignorance, and surely such a "no" should not be allowed to stand forever, once the fullness of the kingdom and its treasures have been revealed.

Or, alternately, sometimes humans say no to God out of anger or rebellion, the way a lover might say "I hate you" to her beloved in the midst of a fight. Again, shouldn't one have the opportunity to repent from such a "no" once the anger has passed and the reconciliation has occurred? Isn't it possible to hold out the hope that such a human "no" might be renounced once the reality of the resurrection and the possibility of new life is finally seen with clear eyes? Somehow, an understanding of Christian salvation must include the reality both of God's "yes" to humanity and humanity's "no" to God.

In summary, in this chapter I noted that because there is no one single doctrine of salvation that has been exclusively endorsed by the Christian church, we must keep a variety of themes and characteristics before us as we consider what the reality of salvation signifies and how it is experienced. In today's twenty-first-century context, any relevant, meaningful doctrine of salvation must take into account one's social and cultural location, it must honor the relationship of humanity to the rest of the physical creation, and it must speak a word of hope to those who are suffering now.

Further, using three different theories of atonement, I suggested three characteristics of God's saving work through Jesus Christ that must be upheld to explain satisfactorily and compellingly how salvation for the whole world can come through the life, death, and resurrection of one individual. To conclude, I outlined five tensions that must be maintained to speak honestly about the dynamic of salvation in the complex context of God's relationship with humanity. It is now time to turn our attention to Buddhism, begin our exploration into a new world, and open ourselves up to new insights and new possibilities.

3

Introducing Buddhism

I take refuge in the Buddha
I take refuge in the Sangha
I take refuge in the Dharma[1]

Buddhism is a rich, wide, and deep religious tradition. Its doctrinal and institutional history spans two and a half millennia, and its tenets have been translated across several linguistic and cultural boundaries in its spread out of northeast India. Given this history, a comprehensive overview is impossible in one short chapter. Thus, this chapter will discuss the origins and developments of the tradition, selectively privileging those that are most important for grounding a dialogue between Christianity and Buddhism.

Keep in mind that the very term *Buddhism* is itself colored by Western prejudices, which favor specific definitions and firm boundaries in order to facilitate religious categorization. Discussing the history and development of the term, Donald Lopez notes in the introduction to *The Story of Buddhism* that, among Buddhists themselves, until only recently there was "little cognizance" of belonging to a pan-Asian religion that

transcends critical national, cultural, and geo-
graphical boundaries.[2] Thus, my description and
definitions in this chapter are admittedly limited
in scope, and they are influenced not only by my
experience as a practicing Christian but also by my
affinity for one particular school of Buddhism (to be
discussed in chapter 4). Every viewpoint has a lens,
and every lens both reveals and distorts its subject
in what it chooses to focus on and what it leaves
fuzzy on the margins of the frame. This chapter is
no different. Nonetheless, keeping these limitations
in mind, the picture of Buddhism presented here is
intended to provide orientation and insight into the
origins and development of Buddhism, as well as a
basis for the more specific discussion of Buddhist
philosophy to come in chapter 4.

Life of the Buddha

When discussing the life of the Siddhartha Gautama, it helps to first know a little about the context into which he was born. Buddhism actually
began in India, a somewhat ironic fact given that
in subsequent centuries it died out there completely, for reasons still debated by scholars. Thus,
the forms of Buddhism practiced in India today
were actually reintroduced from other parts of
Asia, beginning in the nineteenth century.

In his study on Buddhism, Donald Mitchell
notes that "Gautama was born during a historical
epoch when the Indian culture was open to his religious message of enlightenment, compassion, and
peace."[3] The religious landscape of India at this
time was fertile soil for a new religious teaching.
In Hinduism, the recently composed Upanishads

emphasized a move away from the ritual worship of different personal gods and presented a more contemplative path that focused on the mystical union between the individual and an impersonal One, the spiritual reality called Brahman. These texts taught that through meditation and insight, one could realize the truth of this belief and attain liberation, *moksha,* from the endless cycles of suffering and death that characterize human existence in the world, known as *samsara.* This paradigm, in which the individual soul seeks release from the endless cycle of rebirths into a world characterized by change, decay, and illusion, was accepted not only by Hinduism but also by Buddhism and Jainism—both of which developed at this time in India. This move away from a focus on an established structure of ritual and rites, combined with the suspicion some people were feeling toward the priests, who were making a fine living from their participation in these rituals, led many people to leave the cities and reside in forests as "strivers," or *shramanas*—those who were seeking liberation and contentment beyond the temporary pleasures of the world. Into this world of religious and philosophical restlessness, the Buddha, Siddhartha Gautama, was born.

To further set the stage here, let me say a few words about the picture of the universe in Buddhism, as it differs markedly from that found in Christianity. The views of the world espoused by Buddhism, Hinduism, and Jainism are all based on the common cosmology of Indian religious culture, and thus all share a cyclical paradigm for understanding the universe. In Buddhism, the universe has no beginning—it is eternal. In particular, in Indian Buddhism, the universe is said to pass through four stages in unceasing cycles: creation, abiding, destruction, and nothingness. A new cycle of creation is said to begin when "the faint wind of past karma of beings" starts to blow in the nothingness.[4] Beings come into the world during the period of abiding. During the period of destruction, the physical universe is annihilated. Then, at the end of the period of nothingness, the cycle begins again.

The universe consists of six different realms, some of which are more advantageous than others. The highest realm is the realm of the gods, which contains different heavens. Perhaps surprisingly, in Buddhism the gods are still subject to karma and are not immortal. This realm, then, is like a paradise, but it is not *nirvana*; while the gods live very long and enjoyable lives, they will eventually die, and when they do, as typically they have squandered their fortuitous birth in the delight of sensual pleasures, they often will be born into a lower realm. Next is the realm of the demi-gods or "titans"; then the realm of humans, which is, in some ways, the best possible realm in which to be born because there it is possible to be taught the Four Noble Truths; then the realm of animals; then the realm of hungry ghosts; and finally, the lowest realm of hell-beings, a complex and multilayered system comprised of a variety of hells. Every being in *samsara* exists in one of these six realms, and a being's place in a certain realm is due to his or her past karma.

This multilayered universe is pictured in a familiar image called the Buddhist Wheel of Life. In the center of the large wheel are a pig, a rooster, and a snake, which represent ignorance, greed, and

hatred. Each of the six spokes of the wheel represent one of the six realms, and the whole wheel
is clasped by the Lord of Death, symbolizing the
subjection of each being in the wheel, as well as
each realm in the wheel, to the cyclical pattern of
samsara.

The Buddha's Birth

Much contention surrounds the different details of
the Buddha's birth, life, and enlightenment. Certainly, this is in no small part because the first
complete biographies of the Buddha were not
written until hundreds of years after his death, and
they include legends that were not part of earlier texts. Where the earliest texts give only frag-
mentary information about the Buddha himself,
later biographies offer detailed accounts of every
important moment in the Buddha's life—and not
all of the details are the same in every biography.
What follows, then, is a synthesis, one that represents the life narrative of the Buddha as many
contemporary Buddhists understand it.

The Buddha was born sometime in the fifth
century BCE in Kosala, a former Indian state in the
northeastern part of the country, at the foothills
of the Himalayas, which now belongs to Nepal.
Gautama is his family name, and he was born into
the Shakya clan; the name *Shakyamuni*, which is
sometimes used to describe the Buddha in later
Buddhist writings, is Sanskrit for "the wise one/
sage of the Shakyas." His family were warriors
and rulers—members of what has been traditionally has been called the Kshatriya caste—and all
the early texts agree that he enjoyed a pampered
existence in his youth.

Gautama was raised by his father and his step-mother, Mahaprajapati. It is said that his mother, Maya, died seven days after giving birth, and there exist many stories that describe the auspicious nature of his birth. For example, it is said that the whole earth rejoiced at the moment of the Buddha's birth: the heavens were clear, a cool breeze blew, and all types of flowers bloomed in their fullness. It also is said that Maya gave birth standing up, with one arm on a tree branch, after carrying the Buddha for exactly ten months. It was believed that such a sacred vessel as the womb that carried the Buddha could not be used for anyone else, which explains the early and sudden death of the Buddha's mother.

Another important birth story describes how the Buddha himself selected the time and place of his birth as well as the two who would become his parents. It is said that once he had made his decision, his mother fell asleep one night and dreamed that a white elephant, holding a white lotus flower in his trunk, entered her womb from the right side while she was sleeping. When Maya awoke the following day, she asked her advisors to explain the dream to her. They explained that she had, indeed, so conceived a son and that two divergent paths were before him. If he adopted the traditional life of a householder, with a wife and children, he would become a great king. If, however, he adopted the path of a religious teacher, he would become an awakened one who would teach the way of enlightenment and remove the veil of ignorance and suffering from the world.[5]

In response to this prediction, his father told the sages that he wanted his son to become a warrior, a great leader who might one day perhaps even unite all of India. To facilitate this goal, the sages advised him to surround his son with every type of sensual pleasure and luxury and to hide from him anything that might discourage him from following a conventional path of life as a husband and father. Thus, from the moment of his birth, Gautama's parents shielded him from all that is ugly in life, all that is tragic, all that is painful; surrounding him instead with beautiful women, rich foods, luxurious accommodations, and every sort of physical pleasure.

Let me offer an aside at this point. While one might assume that this part of the story has only historical importance—a record of "the road not taken," so to speak—that would miss an important lesson contemporary Buddhists still take from this part of the Buddha's biography. The sensual pleasures with which Gautama was saturated as he grew up, and the real threat they posed to his spiritual quest, emphasize for Buddhists today how easy it is to be diverted from the religious practice of compassion and mindfulness by the many distractions of daily life. Buddhism certainly does not demand monasticism of its followers, and many schools promote the observance of religious practices in the very midst of secular life. However, Buddhism also recognizes that care and attention must be given to one's religious development, as it is all too easy to lose focus and dedication to one's practice in the face of the illusory temptations of the world. Keeping this in mind, let us return to the narrative.

The Four Sights

Immersed in this life of luxury, Gautama grew up and married a woman named Yashodhara. Eventually, they had a son, whom they named Rahula. This name means "fetter," which indicates that already Gautama was feeling torn between his ties to his family and his desire for religious awakening. This desire for a more single-minded religious life grew ever stronger in Gautama, and his dissatisfaction with the sensual pleasures of a wealthy householder grew as well. In the earliest sutras, the story of Gautama's leave-taking from his house is told more simply: he shaved his hair and beard and left his tearful family behind to practice an ascetic lifestyle. However, in later sutras, the story was elaborated into a larger narrative that is now called "The Four Sights." This story tells how Gautama was finally compelled to leave his home and begin his spiritual quest, which is called "The Great Renunciation."

As we have seen, Gautama was bored and dissatisfied with his life in his gilded cage. One day, out on a chariot ride, he went beyond the bounds that his father had marked off for him and he saw an old man. All signs of aging and decrepitude had been hidden from Gautama to this point in his life, so he was shocked and disturbed by what he saw. He asked the chariot driver who the man was and what had caused his miserable condition; Gautama was told that old age is the fate of every person and that no one can escape it. This was the first of the four sights, and it threw him into a deep melancholy.

Later he went on another chariot ride, again going beyond the bounds of his father's watch. On that ride, he saw a severely diseased man, and he realized that no amount of power or wealth can keep disease away. This was the second sight, and it only deepened his misery. Sometime later, he went on a third chariot ride, and this time he saw a corpse for the first time in his life, and he realized that no matter how much pleasure or satisfaction one finds in one's life now, ultimately it will all end in death. This was the third sight. Finally, on the fourth and final chariot ride, he saw a religious hermit practicing meditation. When he asked who this person was and what he was doing, the chariot driver told Gautama that the hermit had left the physical pleasures of the householder's life in order to seek spiritual liberation from all the suffering and sorrow of the material world.

The stories say that this experience of the four sights as Gautama approached his thirtieth birthday created something of an existential crisis, a serious struggle between his attachment to his family and his desire for the wandering life of a religious ascetic. Ultimately, Gautama realized that the superficial pleasures he was enjoying in the palace were only passing and that they could not provide permanent happiness and peace. This, too, is a lesson many Buddhists continue to apply to their own lives today: true contentment cannot be found by immersing oneself in the impermanent world of desire. Instead, it must be sought through the religious life of spiritual enlightenment. After Gautama came to this realization, he took leave of his family and set off on his spiritual quest, called "The Great Renunciation."

The Great Renunciation
After leaving home, Gautama first studied with a series of teachers, all of whom taught different

practices of meditation designed to help one attain the goal of calming the mind and achieving a state of perfect calm and detachment from the world. He mastered all their methods but did not stay with any of them, because he came to realize that each of these forms of practice did not lead to ultimate enlightenment, or *nirvana*.

Gautama then began a program of severe physical austerities, practicing extreme self-mortification in hopes of attaining enlightenment. At this time, five other ascetics joined him who were impressed with his discipline and drive, which also generated many legendary stories. For example, it is said that during this time, "his backbone became like a string of beads, and his buttocks became like the foot of a camel. Taking hold of his body from the front, he found he held it at the back."[6] He was said to have subsisted on only one sesame seed and one grain of rice per day, and the images depicting the Buddha at this time in his life show him to be completely emaciated. For several years, Gautama and his five companions practiced together without any result, and he realized that severe asceticism was not the way to enlightenment—but, then, what was the way? Pondering this question, he remembered a time early on in his youth when he had attained a pleasant, transcendent state of awareness while sitting under a shady tree. He wondered if returning to that state of blissful contemplation might be the key to attaining enlightenment. Realizing that his body was too weak to support such a strenuous mental endeavor, he accepted some milk-rice (or yogurt, in some accounts) from a village girl, thereby officially abandoning his ascetic practice.

This act greatly disappointed the other five ascetics, and they left him to continue their own rigorous form of practice. For the religion that became Buddhism, however, this act had significant, lasting ramifications. As Richard Robinson and Willard Johnson write:

> Gautama's rejection of extreme austerities hinged on a critical moment when he realized that trying to gain liberation by escaping from the body through mortification was as ineffectual as attempting to escape through abstract absorptions. Caught at a dead end, he was able to open his mind to the possibility that physical pleasure of a nonsensual variety was not to be feared, and that it might form the basis for the liberating insight he sought. He went on to recognize that a healthy body is necessary for the development of discernment in order to understand the relationship of body to mind. In so doing, he took the first step on the Middle Way toward Awakening, a way that became a central feature of the Dharma (or doctrine) he later taught.[7]

The Middle Way in Buddhism thus represents the path between the two extremes of self-denial and self-indulgence, between the sensual pleasures of the Buddha's youth and the self-mortification of his ascetic years.

Thus fortified, the Buddha then resolved to sit under what came to be called the Bodhi Tree, the Tree of Awakening near Bodhgaya, vowing to remain there until he attained enlightenment. It would not, of course, be easy. It is said that Mara, the god of desire, could see the ramifications of the Buddha's actions and realized that if he attained enlightenment, he would no longer be bound by craving and thus would no longer be under Mara's control. To prevent this from happening, Mara attempted to distract the Buddha from his meditation.

The stories of Mara's efforts have been greatly embellished over the centuries. It is said that Mara attacked the Buddha with violent storms of mud, live coals, burning ashes, and rocks, but the Buddha continued his meditation undisturbed, turning the storms into showers of blossoms. Then Mara sent his three beautiful daughters—Lust, Thirst, and Discontent—to tempt the Buddha, but he remained unmoved. Finally, Mara gave up, and the Buddha was free to continue his meditations.

In the course of the night, the Buddha had three visions, each of which furthered him on the path from ignorance to awakening. In the first watch of the night, he had a vision of all his past lives, and he became aware of his personal identity as it had been formed through *samsara*, the endless cycle of birth and death. In the second watch of the night, he had a vision of the law of karma, or how living things come into being and then go out of being, rising into a nobler birth or falling into a lower birth as a result of their deeds. And in the third watch of the night, in the hours just before dawn, he became awakened. Many accounts say that what he saw and experienced in these hours was that there is nothing behind this continual coming into being and going out of being—what is often referred to as "the chain of causation." In other words, the world that we think of as "reality" has no eternal, unchanging essence, and there is no fixed, permanent entity that can be called "the self." (We will return to this and other central teachings of the Buddha later in this chapter.)

After he attained enlightenment, the Buddha (as he was now called, meaning the "Awakened One") despaired that there would be anyone who could understand what he had learned, and he did not think he would be able to teach this path of enlightenment to anyone else. However, the Hindu god Brahma came down from heaven and convinced the Buddha that there were, in fact, some who could understand his teaching.[8] The Buddha then went back to his five ascetic companions, who were now residing at a park in Sarnath, near Banaras, and they became his first disciples. It is said that they all also attained enlightenment through his teaching.

The Buddha lived and taught for eighty years and determined for himself when it was time for him to end his life and attain final *nirvana*. This is one account of his final end.

> At the age of 80, the Buddha accepted a meal from a blacksmith, instructing the smith to serve only him and to bury the rest of the meal without offering it to others. The Buddha contracted dysentery shortly thereafter and lay down on his right side between two trees, which immediately bloomed out of season. He instructed the monk who was fanning him to step aside, as he was blocking the view of the deities who had assembled to witness his passing. He asked the 500 disciples who had assembled whether they had any last question or doubt. When they remained silent, he asked a second time, and then a third. He then declared that none of them had any doubt or confusion, and that they all were destined to achieve *nirvana*. The Buddha then entered into

meditative absorption, and then passed into final *nirvana.*[9]

This scene of the Buddha passing into final *nirvana* is one of the most widely depicted in Buddhist art, with the Buddha lying peacefully on his right side, surrounded by all manner of deities, humans, and animals.

Teachings of the Buddha

The heart of the Buddha's first sermon is what has come to be known as the Four Noble Truths. This teaching constitutes the first turning of the wheel of Dharma. These four truths present the Buddha's interpretation of the dissatisfactory human condition and the means by which one can be released from it. In that sense, they are soteriological in intention and they indicate the practical nature of the Buddha's teaching, which is evident throughout the entire canon of Buddhist sutras.

The First Noble Truth: The Truth of Suffering

In the First Noble Truth, the Buddha makes a dramatic, comprehensive statement about the fundamental nature of human life: life the way it is normally lived is suffering. The word in Sanskrit is *dukkha.* Donald Mitchell writes: "The term *dukkha* connotes the dissatisfactory condition caused by an axle hole that is not properly made. Whether the hole is too big or too small, it causes the axle to wobble or rub in a way that is dissatisfactory."[10]

By saying that all life is suffering, the Buddha does not intend to offer a pessimistic view of a horrible world from which one must escape, much less that one must suffer in order to become awakened. Instead, what the Buddha is describing here is the fundamental and most basic consequence of a life lived in ignorance of how things really are. This is what such a life looks like. Typically, humans live their lives attempting to secure happiness for themselves by seeking it in impermanent things—both tangible and intangible—such as money, prestige, beauty, or skill. The reality is, however, that all things change; nothing has permanent, enduring substance. We grow old, people move, relationships fluctuate, our ideas and emotions shift and turn; and so we are constantly disappointed, constantly agitated, constantly unsatisfied. We strive continually after the next best thing, looking for that one final object or goal that will be "enough." However, all is in vain. Permanent happiness, says the Buddha, cannot be found by clinging to the physical and mental things of this world. Such fruitless grasping leads only to restlessness and dissatisfaction. Before we can progress on the path to enlightenment, we must realize this core truth of Buddhist teaching and recognize that the typical way of living can end only in unhappiness.

The Second Noble Truth: The Truth of the Origination of Suffering

In the Second Noble Truth, the Buddha explains how this condition of suffering originates and is perpetuated. According to the Buddha, it is our desire that is the cause of suffering. Thus, the Second Noble Truth states that the cause of our unhappiness and the perpetual state of dissatisfaction with our lives is our craving or "thirst"—the many forms of desire that seek self-gratification in order to find happiness. The most easily recognizable form of this desire is our pursuit of sensual pleasures: food, drink, wealth, and sex. All of these things are impermanent, however, and thus they can never satisfy our desires. Upon reflection, I think most of us can recognize this dynamic in our own lives. For example, after I have bought a new skirt, I want a new sweater; after I have had some ice cream, I want some popcorn; after I get one boyfriend, I want another one; after I get one promotion, I want the next one; after I buy a new house, it suddenly isn't big enough. And so it goes. I exhaust myself trying to satisfy my desire, which is inherently insatiable, and I delude myself by thinking that if I can have just one more, just this one last thing, then I'll be content and my desires will be satisfied.

One scholar describes it this way: "Pleasure is therefore compared to the relief felt when a heavy burden is shifted from one shoulder to another. After a while, the other shoulder will begin to hurt, at which point the burden will be shifted back."[11] Certain things may make us happy for a while, but not for long; and surprisingly quickly, we find ourselves back in the grip of our familiar longing.

The Role of Karma in Buddhist Practice

At this point, it might help to elaborate on the Buddhist doctrine of karma and the role it plays in perpetuating human suffering. A Christian's understanding of karma might well be hampered by the common usage of the term in the West: often, we say that it is "karma" when a person gets repaid in kind for his or her misdeed. So, for example, when a man leaves his wife for another woman who then leaves him for another man, that's karma. In Buddhism, however, karma refers to something much more complex than a simple one-to-one action-reaction relationship. Many Buddhists hold that karma is the driving force behind the cycle of rebirth, which characterizes life for all sentient beings—gods, humans, animals, and demons. According to karma theory, every action has a consequence—good actions generate good consequences, and bad actions generate bad consequences—and these consequences will come to fruition in either this or a future life. Thus, a life characterized by morally good acts will have positive consequences, which ultimately will lead to a better rebirth; bad acts will produce negative results, ultimately leading to a worse rebirth. If one is a human being, a life that has produced good karma will generate a future birth as a better human being—wealthier, happier, more prosperous, and so forth; or perhaps as a god, in one of the heavenly realms of sensual pleasures. However, a life that has produced bad karma will generate a future birth as an animal, perhaps, or even as a hell-being, consigned to one of the hell-realms of suffering and misery. Any individual's current birth, then, is explained by her past karma: she is either reaping the rewards of good karma or being punished for bad karma.

From a Christian standpoint, one of the most difficult aspects of the Buddhist doctrine of karma is that, unlike in Hinduism, there is no permanent, unchanging "self" to be reborn—no "I" that is reincarnated. There are, instead, five constituent parts, or "aggregates," that make up a human person at any given time. These are form, feeling, discrimination, consciousness, and what are called "conditioning factors," a catch-all category that includes things like time and sleep. At death, the temporary bond that has held a specific configuration of these five aggregates together is dissolved, and they come together again in a different configuration in a future birth. One's karma gets lived out in the way in which these aggregates come together in the future.

Another difficult aspect of the karmic cycle for Christians to understand is that, in Buddhism, the goal is to escape karma entirely, not merely to generate good karma. In this process, intention is actually more important than the act itself. Thus it is by the disciplining of one's intention that one is able to perform acts that are without consequence, and thus generate no karma, thereby enabling the practitioner to escape the karmic cycle. Actions and intentions that lead to good karmic consequences still hinder the progress toward enlightenment because they keep one in the karmic cycle: a good rebirth is still a rebirth, still a bondage to illusion.

However, as a penultimate goal, many Buddhists do focus on the production of good karma, and hence on achieving a positive rebirth. One simple reason for this is that one needs good karma to be born into a realm where one is able to hear the teachings of the Buddha and to practice them. This distinction has been described as the difference between "nibbanic" and "kammatic" Buddhisms—the former being the Buddhism of the monastics, who have as their goal the attainment of *nirvana* (*nibbana*), while the latter is the Buddhism of the laity, who have the goal of creating good karma for a better rebirth, one in which it is possible to become a monk and pursue awakening.[12] Finally, it is also important to recognize that, in Buddhism, a good rebirth still leads to temporal happiness—just not to *nirvana*—and so, many Buddhists today also are concerned with generating good karma for its own sake.

The Third Noble Truth: The Truth of the Cessation of Suffering

If these first two truths had been the extent of the Buddha's message, he may well have been seen as a prophet of doom rather than an enlightened teacher of true knowledge. If the Buddha taught only the negative symptoms of human life and offered no way of treating them, it is hardly conceivable that the Buddhist religion would have spread as it did, and developed so rapidly and widely. As it is, however, the diagnosis represents only half of the Buddha's first sermon; the second half is the cure. Thus, the Third Noble Truth offers some hope, as it speaks of the true goal and aim of human life, the attainment of *nirvana*. This truth teaches that the suffering of human existence is not inescapable and that, in fact, an end to such suffering is both possible and attainable. In this truth, then, the Buddha teaches that the cessation of suffering is brought about by a letting go of craving, a letting go of the thirst for more. This leads to the end of suffering, and the realization of *nirvana*.

In Sanskrit, the word *nirvana* literally means "blowing out" or "extinguishing," and it traditionally referred to putting out a fire. For Christians in particular, the word *nirvana* has two common misconceptions associated with it, which must be dispelled. First, in Buddhism, *nirvana* is not a state of bliss, which is how the word is often used in common English parlance. *Nirvana* is explicitly not heaven; in fact, it is not a "place" at all to which one is delivered upon attaining enlightenment. As Donald Lopez writes, "Nirvana is not technically a place but instead an absence, the absence of suffering in the present and the absence of any possibility of suffering in the future."[13] *Nirvana* is not another realm opposed to and entirely distinct from this universe, or even from this life. While the teachings of various Buddhist schools differ somewhat on this last point, it is widely accepted by most Mahayana Buddhists at least that *nirvana* is found right in the midst of *samsara*; and that, when understood rightly, they are simply two different ways of looking at the same reality. I will say more about that shortly.

Second, *nirvana* is not annihilation, as though once one achieves *nirvana* one simply vanishes or ceases to exist. This is another common misunderstanding in the West, where sometimes *nirvana* has been equated with nihilism and nothingness. It is not the self that is extinguished but rather, the false understanding of the self, the delusion that the self is an independent, permanently existing entity. It is not the mere fact of one's existence that leads to suffering; rather, it is the distorted understanding of one's existence and the misguided attempts to fulfill that existence that leads to suffering. Thus, *nirvana* is more properly directed at correcting that distorted understanding and those misguided efforts, not at "destroying the self"—whatever that might mean. As Richard Payne notes, *nirvana* is the cessation of mistaken conceptions and

Right Effort, Right Mindfulness, and Right Concentration. Let me say a bit about each of these
separately.

Right Understanding can be summarized as
the knowledge of impermanence. In other words,
it is the understanding of oneself as one really
is. Right Understanding therefore leads to freedom from ignorance and the realization of the
truth of existence. Right Thoughts are threefold:
the thoughts of renunciation, which keep one
from abandoning oneself to sensual pleasures;
kind thoughts, which are opposed to ill will;
and thoughts of harmlessness and peace, which
keep one from acts of cruelty. Focusing on these
thoughts purifies the mind from corruption and
malevolence. Right Speech points to the act of
refraining from falsehood, stealing, slandering,
harsh words, and frivolous talk. Christians might
here think of the commandment not to "bear false
witness"; something similar is implied here. Right
Action is about refraining from actions that injure
others, such as killing, stealing, and promiscuity.
Practicing this element helps one to develop a
character that is self-controlled and mindful of
the rights of others.

The element of Right Livelihood is very specific
in that it describes five types of employment that
all Buddhists should avoid: trade in deadly weap-
ons, trade in animals for slaughter, trade in slavery,
trade in intoxicants, and trade in poisons. One can
surely think of many "respected" occupations that
would fall into these categories, and one strength
of this element is that it reminds Buddhists that
every aspect of their lives, including their occupation, must conform to the Buddha's values. Simply

put, Right Livelihood means earning one's living in a way that is not harmful to others.

Right Effort consists of the following four aspects: (1) the effort to rid oneself of the evil that has already arisen in one's previous births; (2) the effort to prevent the arising of new evil in one's current birth; (3) the effort to develop the good that has already arisen; and (4) the effort to cultivate the production of good that has not yet arisen. Buddhists believe that effort is needed to cultivate good conduct because humans are so easily distracted and tempted by what is easy and familiar—we keep making the same mistakes over and over just because they are patterns we know. Thus, the Buddha teaches that attaining both happiness and enlightenment requires one's own efforts. No matter how great the Buddha's own achievement was or how excellent his teaching, one must practice that teaching oneself to realize its positive effects.

Right Mindfulness is described as all encompassing, so it includes mindfulness with regard to every aspect of one's being—for example, mindfulness about one's body, including what one is doing physically at any given time; mindfulness about one's feelings and sensations, including what is motivating one's actions and how one might be reacting to people or objects in one's environment; mindfulness about what one is thinking, whether one is focused on negative or destructive thoughts or is caught up in erroneous views; and finally, mindfulness about the world, which includes not getting caught up in illusions about what is real and what is not. Again, simply put, Right Mindfulness is the cultivated practice of awareness of one's deeds, words, and thoughts.

Finally, Right Concentration points to the gradual process of training the mind to focus on a single object and to remain fixed on that object without wavering. Buddhists believe that the consistent practice of meditation helps to develop a calm and concentrated mind, which is a necessary condition for attaining enlightenment. Another way Buddhists have described the purpose and function of the Eightfold Path is by organizing the eight elements into three "trainings": ethics (which includes action, speech, and livelihood), meditation (which includes effort, mindfulness, and concentration), and wisdom (which includes understanding and thought).

Note that the experience of *nirvana* is not the creation of something new in the sense that one must become someone different than he or she was before. A nice analogy that one reads occasionally in Buddhist literature points out that when a person enjoys the freedom of *nirvana,* she is like a lotus flower that rises out of the muddy waters. Freed from the coating of mud that hid her true form, she is free to live unfettered as she really is. Notice that it is the same flower that was there all along—only the mud has been removed to let the true nature of the flower show forth. So also with us. Once our cravings have been removed, our true enlightened nature is able to shine through clearly and we are able to see the world as it really is and ourselves as we really are.

The Three Baskets of the Buddha's Teaching

Buddhism does not have a work comparable to the Christian Bible. While certain schools of Buddhism focus more exclusively on certain sutras, there is no "one book" that serves as a unifying document for all Buddhists. Instead, Buddhism recognizes a wide variety of "teachings" of the Buddha, which typically are organized into three "baskets," called *pitakas*. First is the Sutra Pitaka, which is the collection of the sutras, or sermons of the Buddha. Second is the Vinaya Pitaka, the collection of the Buddha's rules for the monastic community, called the Sangha. These first two baskets of teachings were recorded and collected by the first Buddhist council, held sometime during the year after the Buddha's death. They were recited by the monks closest to the Buddha and then written down and preserved. Finally, the Abhidharma Pitaka is the collection of philosophical reflections on and systematization of the Buddha's teaching that developed in the centuries after his death. These three collections of teachings are the source and norm for Buddhism as a whole, but they are utilized differently and to different degrees in the various Buddhist schools.

The Development of Buddhism

There is no one monolithic Buddhism, just as there is no one monolithic Christianity—or any other religion, for that matter. Buddhism was influenced by the cultures and nations into which it spread, and thus, for example, Japanese Buddhism today has a unique character different from that of Tibetan Buddhism and so on. The differences between the schools of Buddhism throughout Asia and beyond are profound. However, at the same time, there are general characteristics and patterns of development that can be noted.

The Development of Buddhism in India

Since India is the country of the Buddha's birth, and hence also the country in which Buddhism was born, it is important to note both its development and its decline there. Understanding the spread of Buddhism in India is impossible without recognizing the importance of King Ashoka. In 268 BCE, Ashoka inherited an empire that covered most of the Indian subcontinent, with the exception of its very southern tip. Although he was not a Buddhist from birth, it is said that Ashoka converted to Buddhism shortly after ascending the throne. However, it seems that at that point, his conversion was nominal, and he did not actually practice the Buddha's teachings in his own life or in his rule.

All that changed, however, some years later. After Ashoka had been ruling for eight years, he conquered the area of Kalinga, in the northeast of India. The fighting in this battle was particularly bloody, and the carnage particularly devastating. This experience led Ashoka to reflect more deeply on the teachings of the Buddha; it is said that he repented from his violence and vowed to become a different type of king. From this point on, Ashoka began to rule by Dharma, in what is known as his "Dharma conquest." Instead of ruling by force, he ruled by righteousness.

As a result of this commitment, even today Ashoka is famous for his many edicts, which he had carved on rocks, pillars, and in caves, all of which proclaim his rule according to Buddhist Dharma. He demonstrated his compassion for his people in many ways, including building shelters for travelers and hospitals for both people and animals. He even went so far as to make his entire royal household vegetarian, in accordance with the Buddhist doctrine of *ahimsa*—nonviolence and compassion toward all creatures. Legend also says that he opened up the ten original *stupas* (shrines) that contained the relics of the Buddha's body and distributed them to the eighty-four thousand new *stupas* that he built throughout India. Buddhism flourished at this time in India as at no other time in history.

So what happened? From these auspicious beginnings, why did Buddhism eventually die out in India? To this day, scholars do not agree about what caused Buddhism's demise. Certainly, part of the cause can be attributed to Hinduism's assimilation of Buddhism, through interpreting the Buddha as a later *avatar* (incarnation) of Vishnu, one of the central Hindu deities. Another possible cause is the Muslim conquest of India, which caused many monks to flee the country. Without the leadership of the Sangha, the monastic community, Buddhism could not survive. Thus, for a combination of reasons, by roughly the thirteenth century CE, Buddhism no longer existed in India. Ironically, then, the Buddhist communities found in India today were established by Buddhists from other parts of Asia in the nineteenth and twentieth centuries.

The Way of the Elders: Early Buddhism

The earliest form of Buddhism traditionally is called Theravada Buddhism, which means "the way of the elders." It is also called "foundational Buddhism," which in some ways is a more preferable term since it points to a form of Buddhism that includes a variety of early schools that differed in points of doctrine, monastic rules, and textual authority.

Sometimes, in older books on Buddhism, the term *Hinayana Buddhism* is used, but this term is to be avoided. It was developed after the rise of what are called the Mahayana schools; and where "Mahayana" means "greater vehicle," "Hinayana" means "lesser vehicle." Thus, it is a derogatory term.

Several characteristics define these earliest schools of Buddhism. First is the use of the Pali language. The Theravada schools maintained a strict use of Pali as the language of liturgy and scholastic debates because they held that the Buddhist texts preserved in Pali were the most authentic and provided the most reliable record of the Buddha's teachings. The Pali canon of the Buddha's teachings is still held in the highest esteem today. Second is a special emphasis on morality and moral purification. In Theravada Buddhism, high moral standards are demanded of practitioners, the monks most particularly but the laity as well. The morality that is advocated is not only external morality—that is, purity in action, but also inner morality—that is, purity of the mind. Moral purity, then, refers to a twofold process in which unhealthy, impure thoughts are eradicated while, at the same time, healthy, pure thoughts are cultivated. Through mindfulness and concentration, the three root evils of greed, hate, and ignorance are overcome and a state of peacefulness is attained.

The third important characteristic is the path of the solitary *arhat*. An *arhat* is one who has attained the final stage of enlightenment through lifetimes of strenuous, devoted practice. He (more rarely, she) has, through his own efforts, followed the path of the Buddha faithfully and achieved *nirvana*. This path is long and rigorous, and only the most dedicated will walk it to the end. The path of the *arhat* was later contrasted with the path of the bodhisattva, promoted in Mahayana Buddhism (discussed below).

Finally, monasticism is a very important component of Theravada Buddhism. The monks provide both moral and spiritual guidance to the laity, and a well-established and mutually beneficial pattern of interaction exists between the two. For example, in traditional Buddhist societies, the monasteries often had schools where the children could come for their education. Various images of the Buddha also were displayed in the monasteries, so that the laity could come and bring offerings of flowers, food, and incense in order to generate merit for themselves. The laity gave food to the monks, attended Dharma talks, and made monetary donations to the Sangha, all of which encouraged the laity in their pursuit of enlightenment. These acts brought them merit that would not only benefit them in this lifetime but also help them gain a more fortunate rebirth in the next. This relationship continues to be important today.

This form of Buddhism was carried into Sri Lanka around 250 BCE by missionaries sent by King Ashoka. Missionaries were also sent to the area of Southeast Asia that now belongs to Burma (Myanmar) and to Central Thailand. Today this form of Buddhism continues to flourish in South Asia, not only in the countries just mentioned but also in Cambodia, Laos, Sumatra, and Java.

Mahayana Buddhism: The Path of Compassionate Action

As Buddhism began to move into East Asia, certain changes in both doctrine and practice developed. The schools of Buddhism that incorporated these changes came to be grouped under the larger category of Mahayana Buddhism, and the new teachings represented in these schools compose what is considered to be the second "vehicle," the second turning of the wheel of Dharma. It is worth noting, however, that the categories of Theravada and Mahayana were not mutually exclusive in the beginning, and there still is some overlapping between them today. Mahayana Buddhism, then, is not one single school, as Theravada Buddhism is not one single school; rather, the term points to a common emphasis on certain Buddhist beliefs that were elaborated upon in a variety of ways in different Buddhist schools in East Asia in particular. Mahayana Buddhism is the primary form of Buddhism in Tibet, China, Korea, Japan, and Vietnam.

One main source of these changes was new sutras of the Buddha that began to be promulgated around the first century CE. Most scholars agree that these new sutras did not actually date from the time of the Buddha. Instead, it is believed that they were written in Sanskrit from around the first century CE up until the eighth century. Nonetheless, they were accepted by many Buddhists as authentic, and they contain some of the most well-known and best-loved Buddhist texts in the world, including the Diamond Sutra and the Heart Sutra.

These new sutras of the Buddha extolled a new path, a path they claimed was superior to the path of the *arhat* promoted in Theravada Buddhism. The path these new sutras advocated is called the bodhisattva path. It differs from the path of the *arhat* in that it emphasizes taking many lifetimes to attain full Buddhahood in order to devote oneself to helping others attain awakening.

A bodhisattva is one who has vowed to dedicate his or her practice to the enlightenment of all sentient beings. Thus, compassion is at the heart of the bodhisattva path. In this way, the path of the bodhisattva differs from the path of the *arhat*, in which one seeks purification and *nirvana* for oneself. The bodhisattva instead seeks to accumulate merit over countless lifetimes that can be used to help others attain awakening. Instead of seeking release from the endless cycle of *samsara*, the bodhisattva remains in the world of suffering in order to help others awaken. According to Mahayana doctrine, there exists a plurality of bodhisattvas, including the beginners who have just taken the bodhisattva vow as well as the vast array of celestial bodhisattvas who dwell in distant "Buddha fields" and intervene in response to the petitions of living beings in distress. Shakyamuni Buddha remains the paradigmatic "bodhisattva," but as one among others. Human bodhisattvas might be compared to Christian saints, as both are people whose lives are marked by compassion and exemplary ethical behavior.

In addition to the bodhisattva path, Mahayana Buddhism has several other important character- istics. One of the most radical is the concept of *upaya*, "skillful means." This doctrine points to the willingness of the Buddha to do anything, to appear anywhere anytime to teach human beings the truth about reality, thereby leading them to enlightenment. We might think of it as the end justifying the means: whatever the Buddha does, even if it requires illusion, is justifiable as long as it promotes the goal of enlightenment. The Lotus Sutra is one particular sutra in which this doctrine is not only taught but in fact lifted up as central to the right understanding of the Buddha's own teaching and the type of path a Buddhist should follow.

One important ramification of this teaching is that, according to the doctrine of *upaya,* the Buddha was not ever actually a real human being like you and me. Instead, in reality, the Buddha is eternal, "a being who transcends all boundar- ies of time and space, an ever-abiding principle of truth and compassion that exists everywhere and within all beings."[16] He appeared in human form in order to teach human beings the truth about reality, and he entered final *nirvana* in order to motivate people in their own practice to follow him. This understanding of the Buddha, then, led to the teaching of the three bodies of the Buddha, different ways the Buddha manifests himself in the world. The first body of the Buddha—called the "manifestation body," the *nirmanakaya*—refers to the actual, physical, historical body of the Buddha.

The second body of the Buddha—the "enjoyment body," the *sambhogakaya*—refers to the glorified body, the perfected body that the Buddha takes in the various pure lands where he appears to his disciples. Finally, the third body of the Buddha—the "dharma body," the *dharmakaya*—refers to the essential nature of the Buddha, the essential truth at the heart of all reality. As such, it is best thought of as a metaphorical body, the body to which one turns for refuge.

Also important to note in Mahayana Buddhism is what might be called a more elaborate cosmology, a more complex view of the universe. As I noted at the beginning of this chapter, there is a system of karma and rebirth in Buddhism, meaning that upon death one's next birth can take place in a higher or a lower realm, according to one's behavior in this life. In Mahayana Buddhism, what is added to this system is the existence of even higher realms, called "Buddha realms," in which a Buddha resides to help guide his disciples along the path to awakening. This change in cosmology relates to the bodhisattva path, one aspect of which is the belief that by following it, one can be reborn in one of the Buddha heavens, where one can continue to progress toward becoming a Buddha under the guidance of the particular Buddha of that heaven. Naturally, this is the most auspicious birth possible, one that has a much higher chance of success for the disciple. This is logical: the closer you are to a Buddha, the more likely it is that you will attain your goal of enlightenment.

It should also be noted here that in Mahayana Buddhism, once a person attains Buddhahood her- or himself, he or she will create a new Buddha realm of his or her own, in which he or she will help others throughout the cosmos. One way this happens is through what is known as "merit transfer," where the merit that these celestial Buddhas and bodhisattvas have accumulated over countless lifetimes is transferred to needy sentient beings. Another way this happens is through the ability of the various Buddhas and bodhisattvas to appear in different forms at different times and places to help unenlightened beings free themselves from suffering.

Vajrayana Buddhism (Tantric Buddhism): Awakening in This Life

Vajrayana Buddhism represents the last turning of the wheel of Dharma. The word *Vajrayana* means the "diamond" or "thunderbolt" vehicle. Vajrayana is seen as a swift path to enlightenment, in contradistinction to the bodhisattva path or the path of an *arhat*. It teaches that it is possible to become awakened in one's current incarnation; it is not necessary to wait for an optimal rebirth. Enlightenment is attained through the development of specific practices and rituals. One important feature of many schools of Vajrayana that distinguishes them from the previously discussed forms of Buddhism is that a guru or teacher is needed to facilitate proper practice. The rituals are complex—one might even say dangerous—and thus a guru is needed to safeguard the disciple and ensure proper practice.

As I noted above, Vajrayana teaches a relatively quick path to enlightenment, one that can be traversed in one lifetime rather than many. This path encourages a person to see *nirvana* in *samsara*, that is, to see the sacred within the secular rather than apart from it. Vajrayana practice, then, can involve the breaking of traditional Buddhist values and mores, and might include consuming alcohol and rejecting celibacy, for example. Through these practices, one becomes able to see the essence of *nirvana* in all reality, uniting the pure and the impure and dissolving all such distinctions, which are, in and of themselves, inherently artificial. However, it must be definitively stated that Vajrayana practice does not mean that anything goes—it is not a license to do whatever one wants! This is why a teacher is needed: to prevent excesses and to keep the disciple focused on his or her practice.

Doctrinally, Vajrayana espouses many of the same beliefs found in Mahayana Buddhism, such as the bodhisattva path, the role of cosmic Buddhas and bodhisattvas, and the doctrine of emptiness, which will be discussed in detail in chapter 4. This form of Buddhism is dominant in Tibet, and there in particular it is also characterized by the development of a rigorous monastic education, which lasts over a decade and includes the memorization of a copious canon of sacred texts. The debates over points of doctrine within the monastic communities are legendary and are said to have the same drama and excitement of a professional football game in the West.

We come now to the end of this all-too-brief overview of Buddhism. It is my hope that this chapter has provided the proper insight and orientation needed for the following chapter, in which a few key teachings and practices will be elaborated on and related to the unique understanding of soteriology in Buddhism.

4

A Buddhist Understanding of *Nirvana*

W ith its general introduction to the Buddha and Buddhism, chapter 3 laid the groundwork for what now follows: an examination of the concept of *nirvana* and the specific doctrines and practices that attend it. The concept of *nirvana* is much like the concept of salvation in one important practical way: there is no one single understanding or description of *nirvana* to which all Buddhists of every stripe and color subscribe. Instead, different Buddhist schools use a variety of language and images to explain both what *nirvana* is and how one attains it. Again, as with a Christian understanding of salvation, this does not mean that anything goes—the discussion of *nirvana* typically takes place within the bounds set out by the Buddha himself in his own sermons, particularly in the Four Noble Truths—but it does require that, before launching into such a discussion, one needs to be clear about one's sources and perspective.

In this chapter then, I first introduce the figure of Nagarjuna, whose place in Buddhism has been compared to that of Augustine in Christianity and

Moses Maimonides in Judaism. His is the perspective I adopt when describing *nirvana*. Next, I analyze the doctrine of emptiness, or *sunyata*, and the corresponding doctrine of *pratityasamutpada*, which is often translated (somewhat clumsily) as "dependent origination." These two doctrines form the heart of Nagarjuna's understanding of *nirvana* and *samsara*, which refers to the world as we typically experience it. Then I examine what I call different "practices of *nirvana*"—that is, the different means by which Buddhists become awakened to the reality of *nirvana* in their own lives today. I group the four practices of meditation, mantras, mandalas, and monasticism under the larger heading of "mindfulness." In different ways, each of these Buddhist practices contributes to a certain mode of being, a certain relationship to reality, and serves to right one's overall orientation to the world in order to realize *nirvana*.

Nirvana according to Nagarjuna

The Life of Nagarjuna

Nagarjuna commonly is considered the most important teacher in Buddhism after the historical Buddha himself. It is perhaps ironic, then, that few details are known about his life. The particulars of his life and death continue to be debated, but typically Nagarjuna is thought to have been born around 150 CE and to have died around 250 CE. The tradition commonly accepts the fact that he was born into a Brahmin family, but these meager facts are all of the background information on Nagarjuna that can be stated with confidence.

In many biographies, Nagarjuna is said to have had magical powers, thought to be proof of his advanced insight into the truth of existence. One example will suffice. A famous story associated with Nagarjuna is his legendary encounter with the *nagas*, mythical undersea dragons.[1] According to this story, Nagarjuna was lecturing at the Buddhist monastic university of Nalanda, where he was an abbot. Nagarjuna noticed two young men who were frequenting his lectures; whenever they were present, the fragrance of sandalwood filled the entire area, and when they left, the fragrance disappeared with them. When Nagarjuna questioned them, they told him that they were not men at all but *nagas*, and no ordinary *nagas* at that (if there could be such a thing) but sons of the *naga* king.

They told Nagarjuna that centuries earlier, when the Buddha was teaching, the *nagas* also had attended his lectures and had realized that few humans had actually understood their true meaning. Therefore, the *nagas* themselves had written down these advanced teachings of the Buddha and saved them for a time when a person might be born who could understand them. Nagarjuna, they felt, was the one for whom they had been waiting. They then invited him to their kingdom under the ocean to read those sutras, called the "Perfection of Wisdom" sutras because they were believed to be the perfect expression of the Buddha's true teaching. Nagarjuna accompanied them to their undersea world and studied the sutras; after a time, he returned to the human world to teach what he had learned. The name Nagarjuna, then, is believed by many to have come from his encounter with the *nagas*.

Given such illustrious origins, it is perhaps not surprising that one Buddhist scholar has noted that Nagarjuna "was, in short, considered to be the second Buddha,"[2] and that he always figures prominently in the transmission lineages for almost all of the different Buddhist schools in Tibet, China, and Japan. What's more, as the legend reveals, Nagarjuna's interpretation of the Buddha's teaching is accorded the highest authority by many East Asian schools of Buddhism as well. Thus, even in spite of the lack of concrete biographical information about him, enough is known to state with confidence that Nagarjuna is one of the most important early Buddhist thinkers in the tradition. The pervasiveness of his influence on the various schools of later Buddhism is indisputable.

One last point about Nagarjuna himself. While he was an influential philosopher and thinker, he was also a Buddhist monk and thus was heavily involved in the traditional ritual practices and moral codes that governed monastic life. This means, too, that for Nagarjuna philosophy was not an end in itself. It was always directed toward the goal of enlightenment and had a soteriological function. In this regard, his teaching mirrors the Buddha's own.

Nagarjuna's most important work is the *Mulamadhyamakakarika*, or the MMK (as it is typically abbreviated). The name of this text translates roughly to "fundamental stanzas on the middle way." In this work, Nagarjuna emphasizes that he is not teaching any new doctrine but, rather, only expounding on and clarifying the Buddha's own teaching. To do this, Nagarjuna focuses on the Buddha's teaching of the "middle path": in this case, the path between the two extremes of essentialism—believing that reality consists of permanent, unchanging substances (which incidentally modern physics also rejects), and nihilism—the belief that nothing truly exists at all. It is in this framework that Nagarjuna lays out his understanding of the true nature of reality as characterized by emptiness and dependent origination. Once this has been established, Nagarjuna then explains the true nature of both *nirvana* and *samsara*. These explanations laid out in the MMK are superlative.

Sunyata: The Concept of Emptiness

The concept of *sunyata*, most often translated "emptiness," is one of the most well-known Buddhist ideas in the world; many would say that it is one of the, if not the most, important philosophical and religious concepts in Mahayana Buddhism as a whole. Giving just one definition of *sunyata* is difficult, in no small part because the way it has been described by different Buddhist and non-Buddhist scholars throughout the tradition varies greatly. One way to begin a definition of such a multifaceted, complex idea is to describe *sunyata* negatively, starting with what it is not: it is not an object, a thing, a/the Supreme Being, the Absolute, the Void, and so forth. Most important to note for Christian readers, perhaps, is that *sunyata* cannot be personified in the form of a god—in fact, it cannot be personified in any way. Emphasizing this point, one commentator writes that to identify *sunyata* with some form of absolute is "as if a shopkeeper were to say, 'I have nothing to sell you,' and would receive the answer, 'Very well, then just sell me this—your absence of goods for sale.'"[3]

However, this does not mean that there are no positive statements that can be made about *sunyata*. For Buddhists, *sunyata* represents the true form of existence, the state in which all things "are." Further, and perhaps most importantly, emptiness is the key to enlightenment, the key to freeing oneself from suffering. An experientially based understanding of emptiness is the wisdom that leads to liberation. Without a proper understanding of *sunyata*, the world will never cease to delude and tempt the individual, and she will never be able to get beyond her simple sense perceptions and desires. Her suffering will never end; nor will she ever escape the karmic bonds that propel her through cycle after cycle of existence. Thus, for anyone who seeks wisdom, the first and most important concept that must be grasped is emptiness.

So, what is it, exactly? Roger Jackson defines *sunyata* as well as anyone. He writes:

> *Philosophically*, emptiness is the term that describes the ultimate mode of existence of all phenomena, namely, as naturally "empty" of enduring substance, or self-existence (*svabhava*): rather than being independently self-originated, phenomena are dependently originated (*pratityasamutpada*) from causes and conditions. Emptiness, thus, explains how it is that phenomena change and interact as they do, how it is that the world goes on as it does. *Religiously*, emptiness is the single principle whose direct comprehension is the basis of liberation from samsara, and ignorance of which, embodied in self-grasping (*atmagraha*) is the basis of continued rebirth—hence suffering—in samsara.[4]

Basically, what Jackson points to first is the theoretical meaning of the term *emptiness*, which is that everything that is, is "empty" of independent, eternal, autonomous substance and existence. Simply put, this definition points to the reality that everything is constantly in flux, changing from moment to moment based on interaction with other beings; that, in fact, all things are actually created through those interactions.

Let me give an example to clarify. Perhaps all of us have experienced at one time or another the unsettling realization that no two people experience or even see the same event the same way: if ten people witness an accident, ten different accounts—sometimes with startling variance—will follow. The "true nature" of that event, then, is not frozen in time, permanently accessible and possessing the same meaning for everyone. Instead, its meaning and true nature are constituted by the participation of all the individuals involved and may well change each time the story is told. Our own history bears this out, as the meaning and interpretation of the very same events can change radically from the perspective of ten years versus fifty or one hundred years. This is the theoretical meaning of emptiness: not that things do not actually exist but that, lacking any permanent essence, their meaning and true nature are always evolving.

This leads to the second part of Jackson's definition, the religious meaning of emptiness. He points out that for Buddhists, understanding this central insight is the key to unlocking the door to *nirvana*. Once the empty nature of existence is truly understood, the root cause of suffering vanishes and one is liberated from the cycle of fruitless grasping after people, things, and ideals—none of which have permanent existence and thus certainly cannot satisfy one's desires.

Let me offer another brief example by way of explanation. The primary cause of suffering is desire, as described in chapter 3. Buddhists assert that because we do not understand the true nature of reality, we believe that having certain things—fame, money, power; or being certain things—a husband, a mother, a monk, or a CEO—will bring us permanent happiness. This is, of course, not the case, because the fact is that none of these things is static, and thus all of them change over time and can be removed or taken away overnight. Just as it is fruitless to try and seal in a box the blowing wind, the falling rain, or the shifting sand, so, too, is it fruitless to try to possess happiness through the attainment of some external "thing" that will not, and cannot, last forever. This realization is at the heart of liberation.

Given the relationship between emptiness and the nature of *nirvana* in the Buddhist tradition, the soteriological efficacy of the Buddha's teaching depends on the proper view of *sunyata*. Hence, emptiness and its complement, *pratityasamutpada*, are the heart and soul of the entire Buddhist worldview and the center of its soteriological path.

Pratityasamutpada: The Doctrine of Dependent Origination

To understand the concept of dependent origination, *pratityasamutpada*, in Nagarjuna's thought, it is first necessary to describe the relationship between *pratityasamutpada* and *sunyata*. In the

MMK, Nagarjuna argues that there is no difference between understanding an entity as "empty"
and understanding it as "dependently arisen."
Both terms point to the same reality. What this
means is that the mode of being in the world
for any entity can be described in two equally
accurate ways. Either one can say that all things
exist in relationship to other things and that those
relationships are constitutive of their being—that
is, nothing can exist on its own, independently:
no man (or woman) is an island; nothing comes
from nothing; every effect has a cause. There is a
complex, vast interconnected matrix of being in
which and out of which everything that is finds
existence. That is the definition of *pratityasamutpada.* Or, one can say that nothing exists fully
independently, completely autonomously, and
exclusively in and of itself. (The technical Buddhist term for this is *svabhava.*) Nothing that
is possesses a static, permanent, unchangeable
nature. Rather, everything is empty of independent, autonomous existence. That is the definition
of *sunyata.*

Either way, the same thing is asserted. Contrary to
the traditional way of understanding phenomena in
Western philosophy, in which independent entities
are considered primary and the relationships between
them only secondary, according to the doctrine of
emptiness, relationships are primary for existence,
and a permanent, autonomous, independent entity
as such does not exist. Thus, *pratityasamutpada* and
sunyata are not two different things but, rather, two
ways of describing the same thing.

Nagarjuna gives several examples to explain
what he means by *pratityasamutpada.* One of the

most easily understood uses the parent-child relationship. Nagarjuna writes: "A father is not a son, a son is not a father. Neither exists without being correlative."⁵ This is obvious to us from our own experience. The assertion that a man is a father requires that he have a child—*father* is a term of relationship, and one cannot attain it independently. At the same time, in that relationship, there is only one father and only one son. Just because each is dependent on the other does not mean that they are interchangeable. Dependence does not mean equivalence.

This example is particularly revealing because it indicates the depth to which these relationships are fundamental to our being. The relationship a father has to his child profoundly changes his entire life. It is not just something "added on" to his "true self," which makes only a superficial change—like a coat of paint that makes the outside of the house look nicer but doesn't alter the floorplan or the foundation. Rather, the very "selfhood" of a father is reconfigured and re-created by the event of having a child, so much so that he cannot conceive of himself outside that relationship. In just this way, says Nagarjuna, the entire world is interdependent and interrelated—we just fail to realize it.

Another example Nagarjuna uses is that of a medicine. He writes: "No medicine appears independently of its specific ingredients. It appears [like] an illusory elephant: It is not [identical with them] nor is it [absolutely] different from them."⁶ Here, Nagarjuna points out that an efficacious medicine requires the combination of specific ingredients, none of which is therapeutic on its own. It is impossible to isolate one component of any medicine and pronounce that it, and it alone, is the one individual healing property of the medicine. The medicine works only insofar as it combines a balance of ingredients. The medicine is not this or that ingredient but, rather, the unique combination of all of the ingredients together. Yet, it is the combination in active relationship that is medicinal: a bunch of ingredients all piled up loosely on a counter does not constitute a medicine. A medicine is not a mathematical equation, in which one apple plus two oranges plus three bananas makes six pieces of fruit. Medicine does not result from the static combination of discrete, autonomous objects, but rather depends on a series of specific, dynamic relationships.

In his teaching and his writing, Nagarjuna describes a world in which everything is dependent on everything else, and therefore also empty, empty of any permanently abiding essence. These two ideas, which seem in direct contrast, actually point to the same reality.

Nirvana and *Samsara*

In the MMK, Nagarjuna writes: "There is no distinction whatsoever between samsara and nirvana. There is no distinction whatsoever between nirvana and samsara" (MMK 25:19). This verse is one of the most surprising, controversial verses in the entire work. It is entirely unexpected and challenges much of traditional Buddhist thinking about the nature of *nirvana*. Rather than stress the difference between *nirvana* and *samsara*, Nagarjuna is arguing their lack of distinction. Jay Garfield calls it "one of the most startling conclusions of the *Mulamadhyamakakarika*," and describes Nagarjuna's position as follows: "There is no difference in entity between nirvana and samsara; nirvana is simply samsara seen without reification, without attachment, without delusion."[7] This conclusion certainly warrants more explanation!

The Buddhist concept of *nirvana* commonly is interpreted as an escape from here to there—a turning of one's back on this life and looking elsewhere. This conception of *nirvana* is most prevalent in Western popular parlance, where the very word *nirvana* has come to mean a state of sheer bliss, some otherworldly frame of mind or being. However, such an interpretation does not represent the dominant understanding of *nirvana* in Buddhist thought. Instead, as Nagarjuna describes it, *nirvana* actually consists of the proper insight and perspective into life right here and now. It is in no way to be understood as the end of this life or a rejection of it. Rather, it is the realization of the way things really are, right here and now. In other words, there is no "there" there; instead, *nirvana* is "right here"—suddenly apparent with a shift in perspective or focus. As Garfield says: "Nagarjuna is emphasizing that *nirvana* is not someplace else. It is a way of being here."[8]

In *The Buddhist Concept of Hell*, Daigan Matsunaga uses an analogy that Christians can perhaps appreciate. He argues that, in Nagarjuna's view, "the ultimate difference between heaven and hell lies in the attitude of the viewer."[9] Now, this is not to say that suffering is not real and that some conditions of existence are not better or more felicitous than others. Buddhists are not unsympathetic to genuine suffering, nor are they unmoved by love and joy. However, Buddhist doctrine recognizes that, for many of us, the determinations of "bad" and "good" we apply to certain people and situations are subjective judgments, based solely on our relationship to them, and how we experience them. To a farmer hoping for a good crop, a rainy day is a blessing; for a baseball team hoping to win a tournament, it is a curse. The rain itself is neither good nor bad; there are only good or bad relationships to it. To the person trying to make a connection, a delayed flight is a nightmare; to the person stuck in traffic and running late, it is a godsend. The flight itself just is; it is a person's relationship to it that gives it meaning one way or the other. As Bruce Matthews writes: "The world in itself ought not to be viewed as either a source of pain or not a source of pain. It is only our relation to it through consciousness that makes it thus or otherwise."[10]

Hence, *nirvana* is not a different place other than this world we live in right now. Instead, what is different is our disposition toward it and our understanding of it. The term *samsara* refers to our unenlightened, unawakened view of and relationship to the world; the term *nirvana* refers to an understanding of the world as it truly is and living accordingly.

One important caveat must be noted: for many lay Buddhists all over the world, rebirth in a higher realm—rather than realizing *nirvana*—has been the primary religious goal.[11] As Donald Lopez notes: "Despite repeated admonitions that birth as a god is a temporary state from which one must eventually fall, to be reborn in a lower realm . . . a happy life and an auspicious rebirth have remained goals more sought after than escape from samsara into nirvana. Indeed, much Buddhist literature intended for both monks and lay people has promoted a social ideal, defining the good life and explaining how to lead it."[12] I note this only as a reminder that while many Buddhists strongly emphasize the soteriological value of the Buddha's teaching on *nirvana*, many other Buddhists focus their practice on more tangible goals, in particular on a propitious rebirth in one's next life.

Buddhist Practices of *Nirvana*

Different Practices of Mindfulness

Considering all that has been said above, particularly given the relationship between *nirvana* and *samsara*—that is, there is no ontological difference between them but, rather, they refer to two different ways of viewing the same reality—I think it is both helpful and accurate to organize this section around the concept of mindfulness. I am using the term *mindfulness* here in its most general sense—the sense of being present to the actuality of one's existence. However, this is not the only way mindfulness is described. It also has a technical meaning, referring to one kind of Buddhist meditation, a kind that has become very well-known in the West. Further, mindfulness is one of the components of the Eightfold Path, the means by which *nirvana* might be realized. In that context, mindfulness is described as "the cultivated practice of awareness of one's deeds, words and thoughts." Nevertheless, in this chapter the practice of mindfulness primarily is used more broadly as an overarching concept that incorporates a wide variety of practices aimed at awakening.

According to Thich Nhat Hanh, a Vietnamese Zen monk and a prolific writer well-known to many Christians, mindfulness refers to "keeping one's consciousness alive to the present reality."[13] In his book *The Miracle of Mindfulness,* he offers several concrete, mundane examples of what this looks like in practice; for example, it means eating with awareness and paying attention as food is tasted, chewed, and swallowed, rather than unconsciously going through a bag of popcorn while watching TV; it means being aware of the feel of the soap and the water and carefully handling every cup while washing dishes in the sink, rather than racing through the task carelessly while thinking about one's plans for the evening; and finally, it means focusing one's full attention on one's partner or child when she or he is talking, rather than listening with one ear while reading a magazine. Most of us, I am sure, recognize ourselves in the "rather" clauses of those sentences. While mindfulness is a concept we may know in theory, it is something we may rarely take the time to practice.

Part of the reason for this is the difficulty inherent in cultivating true mindfulness: it is not easy to give anyone or anything our full attention, as there are always distractions—either from our own thoughts or from the outside world. Even if sometimes we are mindful in a situation that is important to us, such as a job interview, a first date, or a sports performance, this practice is certainly more the exception than the rule. And make no mistake, what is meant by mindfulness in Buddhism is more than simply being a little more focused once in a while. Instead, it is a comprehensive discipline that incorporates all of who we are and all of what we do—our actions, our thoughts, and our breath.

The reason mindfulness is such a central Buddhist practice is that ignorance lies at the heart of suffering—in particular ignorance about the true nature of reality. It is ignorance that drives us to thirst for fleeting things that cannot make us happy; and it is ignorance that veils the true nature of the universe, the fundamental interconnectedness that characterizes all that is. Without the practice of mindfulness, then, our ignorance will continue, and we will keep on striving fruitlessly after false desires, blinded by a deluded sense of egoism.

However, with discipline, concentration, and awareness, we are able to free ourselves from these false delusions and uncover what too often passes right by us unnoticed. In this way, we move—either gradually or all at once—from ignorance to wisdom, from illusion to reality, from confusion to clarity; also, therefore, from anxiety to calm, from restlessness to peace, from perpetual dissatisfaction to contentment. This state of awareness and peace is the difference between *samsara* and *nirvana* and is the key to awakening.

Perhaps the most familiar entry to the world of Buddhist practice is the idea of meditation. While the practice of meditation by laity actually is a modern phenomenon, it is commonly understood by Westerners as the defining characteristic of Buddhism. As such, we will explore it first but then go on to discuss some other representative forms of Buddhist practice—mandalas, mantras, and monasticism, the latter being one of the most important forms of religious practice in Buddhism as a whole.

Meditation: Concentration, Contemplation, Visualization

Paul Griffiths notes that "meditational practice has always been of central importance to Buddhist soteriology and Buddhist philosophical theory."[14] All the more reason then, that here, at the beginning of a discussion of the practice of meditation in Buddhism, several cautions must be noted. First, many Christians, when they hear the word *meditation*, think of closing their eyes, forgetting all the worries of the day, calming down, and relaxing. In many ways, then, in the West, meditation is looked upon as an "anti-practice"—more of a not-doing, not-thinking, not-rushing—rather than a disciplined practice with positive content in its own right. Second, many Christians associate meditation with prayer and think of meditation as another way of being in communication with God. In this light, a variety of metaphors are often used for meditation: listening for God, waiting for God, opening oneself to the presence of the Spirit, and so forth. While there is nothing inherently wrong with either of these interpretations from a Christian point of view, neither one is appropriate when trying to understand meditation in the Buddhist tradition. Therefore, it is necessary for Christians to put aside any preconceived notions of what meditation is or is not, and learn about the practice anew from a Buddhist perspective.

Meditation is a deceptive term because, while it suggests something very simple and easy to explain, in actuality Buddhism is filled with many texts that describe the practice of meditation in extreme complexity, with great philosophical sophistication. In fact, an expression frequently encountered in Buddhist literature, "84,000 dharma doors," points to the manifold ways of entering into the experience of enlightenment.

In light of this complexity, then, as a way of making a general introduction to the different types of meditation, I will describe briefly the three types of meditation practice referenced in the heading to this section. First, concentration practices guide the meditator to focus attention on one specific aspect of the immediate experience, such as the Zen practice of focusing attention on the breath. Other objects of concentration include visual objects (a blue circle, for example) and auditory objects (a repeated word or phrase, which will be discussed more fully below).

Second, contemplation practices often are seen as a second stage of the developing meditative practitioner's skill; having learned to focus on some specific, immediately present sensory object, the mind is now "relaxed" and attention is opened to a wider range of the experienced whole of the present moment.

Third, visualization practices engage the practitioner in creating an internal, mental "world" usually accessed through an active process of creating an inner visual image. Some such practices are relatively simple—for example, concentrating on a literal blue circle is followed by forming a mental image of that blue circle. Others are very complicated practices in which the practitioner creates an internal image of a Buddhist deity, including all of the accompanying iconographic details.

Meditation has been called "the heartbeat" of Buddhism, and few would dispute that the various practices of meditation are foundational to the Buddhist life. Meditation involves wisdom and compassion, the two central components of the path of enlightenment, and it is a primary means by which one shakes the hold of ignorance, greed, and anger. The goal of meditation is the realization of *nirvana*, but that in itself does not tell the whole story. Instead, the practice itself—the means, if you will—is also an important component of the goal: the change in one's engagement with the world and in one's understanding of reality and oneself. Paul Griffiths writes, "Meditation on items of Buddhist doctrine is meant to result . . . not only in knowledge that certain things are true, but also in the alternation of the practitioner's cognitive and perceptual experience to accord with that knowledge."[15] In other words, the practice of meditation results in both intellectual understanding of truth and the experiential realization of that truth for oneself in one's own life.

Unsurprisingly, perhaps, there is not one single Buddhist description of a definitive, universal form of meditation for all Buddhists in all times and places. Instead, there exists in Buddhism a wide variety of texts that offer a corresponding variety of forms of meditation. So, for example, in Indian Buddhism, we find over forty subjects of meditation, ranging from concentration on simple, concrete objects, which helps to develop one's concentration, to visualization of corpses in varying stages of decay, which serves to remind the practitioner of the inevitability of death and the impermanence of all life. Different practices are suggested based on one's character and on the particular state of one's religious development.

Contrary to popular belief, most Buddhist texts recognize that meditation is a technical skill to be learned, practiced, and developed, akin to learning to play the piano; and for almost no one is the practice natural and innate. Much as the beginning pianist starts by playing scales, so also the novice begins by practicing an awareness of her breath, which is much harder than one might imagine!

It is also important to recognize that many of the texts that discuss meditation emphasize attentiveness to one's entire physical condition including, of course, one's posture, recognizing that the mind and the body do not work independently and that the state of the latter affects the state of the former, either for good or for ill. So, for example, one work notes the following:

> Now after closing the windows of the senses with the shutters of mindfulness, you should know the proper measure of food that is conducive to meditation and good health. For too much food obstructs the flow of one's breathing, leads to lethargy and sleep, and saps one's strength. And just as too much food produces purposelessness, the consumption of too little food is debilitation. For excessive fasting takes away from the body its substance, its glow, its vitality, its ability to act, and its strength. . . . Thus, as a practitioner of meditation you should feed your body not out of desire for food or love of it but solely for the purpose of subduing hunger.[16]

This idea of a "middle way" between indulgence and asceticism should be familiar; the Buddha himself adopted such a path before he began the meditation that led him to realize *nirvana*.

One of the most well-known schools of Buddhism in the West is Zen Buddhism, and it is primarily through Zen that the Buddhist practice of meditation has been brought into the public eye. Therefore, I will give a brief description of meditation as it is practiced in the Zen tradition, in order to provide a concrete example of what meditation looks like "in action." Those familiar with Zen may know the term *zazen*, which refers to a specific type of seated meditation. In this type of meditation, one sits on the floor, on a cushion, in full lotus pose (when possible), with each foot resting on the opposite thigh. The spine is straight, with the left hand resting on top of the right, and the upper body is relaxed but not slumping.

As this posture is being maintained, one is asked to focus on one's breathing—not counting breaths necessarily but saying, "Now I am breathing in one breath" and "Now I am breathing out one breath." As one breathes, one is to feel the breath enter and leave the body and to allow the mind to follow the breath. Instead of trying to fix one's mind on something and hold it there, Zen practitioners are encouraged to observe everything as it happens—to be aware of the random thoughts that cross one's mind and to be aware of the various discomforts of one's body—but then to let them go, not clinging to them, so that thoughts, just like the breath, flow in and out of one's mind naturally. And that is the essence of the practice—but rest assured, fruitful practice is much harder than it sounds!

Through this deceptively difficult exercise, one experiences one's true nature, which is also called "Buddha nature," and develops the ability to express this nature not only while in sitting meditation but also while engaged in the daily activities of one's life. In this way, the practice becomes an end in and of itself and not simply the means to something else. In other words, meditation becomes an experience of *nirvana*.

Mandalas

Let me begin this section with one simple definition of a mandala: "a circular diagram that contains images of a deity in his or her celestial realm, along with symbols and images that depict enlightened virtues associated with the deity and that indicate core Buddhist ideas and ideals."[17] These mandalas play an important role within Tibetan Buddhism in particular, a form of Buddhism known in the West primarily through the Dalai Lama, a Nobel Prize winner and the spiritual leader of Tibet. It is also accurate, however, to say that mandalas are part of what is called "tantric" Buddhism: that is, practices and doctrines that have their origins in India and were transmitted more or less in secrecy from teacher to student. This and other tantric practices continue to be important in many different Buddhist schools today, and they typically can be recognized by the use of some kind of initiation rite, an emphasis on a personal relationship with a teacher, and some level of secrecy.

You may, at some point, have seen a mandala and simply not recognized it for what it was; to the uninitiated eye, it looks like a complicated abstract pattern with a seemingly random assortment of colors, figures, and symbols—visually dazzling but entirely incomprehensible. However, as I hope to show, strict rules and guidelines govern every aspect of a mandala, from its design to its painting to its dismantling.

Typically, mandalas are two-dimensional; however, they can also be constructed in three-dimensional form or painted. Mandalas vary greatly in scope and design, depending on the deity or deities depicted, which is why there is no one single mandala pattern that is simply replicated in every context. Regardless of the specifics, however, each mandala represents a sacred space, a reality that is, in actuality, more real than this world; and through the practice of visualization, one is able to realize this alternate universe and experience oneself as a part of it.

One important function of a mandala, then, is to invite the practitioner into a divine abode, thereby encouraging in him or her the positive characteristics of the deity, typically a specific Buddha or bodhisattva who is represented in the mandala. To the enlightened one, there is no difference between one's own true nature and the "Buddha nature." By bringing one into the realm of a specific Buddha or bodhisattva, one is able to visualize oneself as possessing this perfected nature and having an awakened mind. It is believed that this experience of visualization will facilitate one's realization of *nirvana*.

Perhaps a point of comparison here might be illuminating, as long as one is careful not to overstate the case. Some general similarities exist between the place and function of mandalas in Buddhism and the role of icons in Orthodox Christianity. Like a mandala, an icon is not simply a picture of something; one common definition of an icon is "a window into heaven," and it is believed that meditation on an icon deepens one's awareness of God's presence. It is also believed by some

Christians that meditating on an icon of a specific saint will help them to develop similar qualities of love and zeal for the faith. Further, an icon is not so much drawn as it is written, and very defined rules govern the materials used and the style of writing. As with mandalas, individual creativity is neither desired nor encouraged.

As a specific example of what a mandala is, I will briefly describe the Kalachakra mandala (the "wheel of time" mandala), which accompanies the Kalachakra initiation that the current Dalai Lama has now conveyed on hundreds of thousands of people. The initiation itself is an empowerment ritual that takes roughly two weeks and culminates in a viewing of the mandala and a blessing by the Dalai Lama. Understandably, only the barest outline of a description is possible here, and I confine my discussion to the mandala itself rather than to the full process of initiation.[18] The creation of the Kalachakra, or any other sand mandala, is a very special kind of ritual event that is worth describing for that fact alone. Understanding the process of creation is also, however, a way to see the practice of mindfulness in action. Buddhist art traditionally has been created by monks and has therefore been seen as providing an opportunity and an encouragement for mindfulness.

Typically, it takes as many as sixteen monks a total of six days to create the mandala. Before they begin, the site must be purified and consecrated. The outline of the mandala is first drawn in chalk, using particular lines of string to ensure precision and accuracy. At several points, the specific deities of the mandala are invoked and invited to take up residence there. Once these rites are completed, the actual applying of the sand begins. The monks work from the inside out, and the design on each side always faces the center. It should be noted that, as part of their training, the monks memorize every detail of the mandala, which is based on Buddhist scriptures. Typically, monks must study several years before they are allowed to participate in the creation of a mandala. Further, as I mentioned above, there is no innovation or creative variation to the design. In fact, the efficacy of the mandala is dependent on its exact replication of the proper specifications.

The monks use a specific tool called a *chakpur*, a long narrow funnel through which the grains of colored sand are distributed. The grains are released through the vibrations of one *chakpur* on the other, and the hole through which the grains fall varies in size based on the degree of precision needed in any given part of the design. When seen up close for the first time, it is almost impossible to believe that such detail could be achieved simply with sand; and the very construction of the mandala demonstrates the monks' patience, wisdom, and insight. When finished, this particular mandala looks like a series of nesting squares, each of which is surrounded by a variety of syllables, symbols, animals, gates, and colored dots, which represent the various deities. One could gaze upon it for hours and not come close to exhausting all of its meaning. A mandala of this scope is truly awe inspiring and a wonder to behold.

Once the initiation is complete, the mandala is dismantled. After the presiding monk is sure that the deities have left the abode, major lines are cut through the mandala, and then all the sand is swept together and put into a vase, where it is carried to a local lake, river, or ocean and poured in with special prayers and offerings. Some sand is also distributed to participants as a sign of blessing.

It is believed that the mandala not only promotes the well-being of those immediately involved in the ritual but it has a more cosmic positive impact as well. The Dalai Lama has said that the Kalachakra mandala and initiation is a vehicle for world peace, and that it benefits the entire community in which it is given. This insight is an important reminder that Buddhism is not a religion that retreats from the world or rejects it. Instead, many Buddhists use their faith as a platform from which to engage the world constructively, working for peace, justice, and greater compassion for all living things. This is especially true for those who call themselves "engaged Buddhists" and see Buddhism as a powerful force in the world, not simply for personal transformation but also for social change on a global scale.[19]

Mantras

In a Western context, the word *mantra*, like the word *nirvana*, suffers from a distortion of its true meaning. Many in American society, for example, think of a mantra as a short saying that one uses for positive reinforcement: "I am a good person"; "I can do it if I try"; or "If I dream it, it can happen." The "I" in each of these sayings is revealing, as it demonstrates that, for many, a mantra is a self-promotional tool used exclusively for one's own betterment. In this usage, mantras are primarily individualistic and insular. This is quite different from the use of mantras in Buddhism.

Like mandalas, mantras also have their origin in Indian tantric practices; along with *mudras*—specific hand gestures and body postures—they were used in a variety of Indian religious contexts as a part of meditative visualization to facilitate one's spiritual liberation. This includes early Buddhism; the Pali canon records several instances in which the Buddha teaches a mantra—including one for protection from snakes—to his followers. The role of mantras is greatest, however, in different schools of Mahayana Buddhism, where mantras are an important means through which various celestial Buddhas and bodhisattvas are called upon for aid. In this context, a mantra can function as a powerful invocation that is addressed to a specific Buddha or bodhisattva. The mantra is repeated over and over in order to deepen one's connection to that figure and to actualize the qualities possessed by him or her, such as wisdom or compassion. One of the most well-known mantras is *Om Mani Padme Hum,* which means something like "O Jewel in the Lotus." It is an invocation to the great bodhisattva of compassion, Avalokiteshvara.

Mantras are particularly important in several schools of Japanese Buddhism, specifically those that have their roots in the Tendai school. The reason for this is that Tendai, as it was founded in Japan by Saicho (in roughly the early ninth century CE), combined traditional practices of meditation with various tantric practices, including the use of mantras. The three major schools of Buddhism that developed out of the Tendai tradition are Zen, Pure Land, and Nichiren Buddhism, all of which are still very influential today, both in Japan and beyond. From these, I would like to use the role of mantras in Nichiren Buddhism to give one concrete example of their function and purpose.

Nichiren was born in the early thirteenth century CE. He is said to have been concerned with religious questions at an early age. As he developed in his study of Buddhism, he became convinced that the Lotus Sutra was the most perfect example of the Buddha's true teaching. Consequently, he rejected all other forms of practice save that which was centered around this particular sutra. The Lotus Sutra is relatively late in composition (middle to late third century CE), but it became popular very quickly—and remains so today—primarily because it promises enlightenment to everyone, teaching that everyone is capable of becoming "Buddha-like" by manifesting one's inherent Buddha nature. Thus, the primary practice that Nichiren developed and taught to his followers was chanting a form of the title of the Lotus Sutra as a mantra: *namu myoho renge kyo,* which can be roughly translated, "Praise to the scripture of the lotus of the wonderful law."

Nichiren believed that this act of praise to the sutra, and thus to the teaching it holds, made the saving power inherent in the Lotus Sutra itself present and effective in the life of the practitioner. To this end, Nichiren said: "If you want to be free from the sufferings of birth and death that you have undergone since beginningless time, and if without fail you want to attain supreme Awakening in this very lifetime, then you must realize the inherent, original perfect truth in all living beings. This truth is *Myohorengekyo.* Therefore, chanting *Myohorengekyo* will enable you to realize the innate perfect truth in all life."[20]

Belief in the power of the Lotus Sutra was reinforced through the centuries in no small part through the repetition of wondrous stories that described the protective power of the Lotus Sutra in action. One example will suffice. In one story from Japan, a Japanese monk had memorized the entire sutra with the exception of two words, which he consistently forgot. Finally, he had a dream in which a man told him that in his past life he had been reading the sutra by the fire and an ember from the fire had jumped out and burned the scroll, obliterating the very two words he was now unable to remember. The monk had died before he repaired the scroll, and the man in the dream told him that unless he fixed the scroll, he would never be able to remember the sutra. He went back to his former home, found the scrolls and repaired it; and was promptly able to recite the sutra in full.[21] Richard Payne notes, "Clearly a text that . . . can reach across lifetimes to enable its devotee to repair a copy . . . is a powerful text."[22] This is only one example of many that illustrates the power mantras possess and their ability to protect, preserve, and transform, enabling one to realize a new way of seeing and engaging the world.

A very superficial comparison can be made here with the Christian practice of centering prayer. In this practice, some Christians use a word such as *love* or *peace* as a way of focusing their minds while praying. However, there are important differences as well. In the Christian practice, this word is not repeated over and over; nor is it meant as an invocation of the presence of God. Instead, it is a tool that the Christian uses to draw the mind back to God when it starts to wander. By contrast, in Buddhism the mantra actually brings into being that which it vocalizes; in the case of the Lotus Sutra, it is the realization of one's true nature and liberation from a false sense of self. Thus, in Buddhism, the recitation of a mantra is a practice that not only focuses the mind but brings about a change in one's whole being.

Monasticism: The Sangha

In almost all schools of Buddhism, the monastic community plays a central role, although there are important differences in practice and identity rooted both in doctrinal interpretation and socio-national context. As noted earlier, monasticism is so important for Buddhism that the Sangha is considered one of the "Three Jewels" in which a Buddhist takes refuge. In fact, it is said that without a community of monks, there can be no Buddhism.

The monastic community in Buddhism grew out of the Indian tradition of wandering ascetics, individuals who were searching for religious truth, eschewing the life of a householder in favor of a life focused on religious pursuits. Following this custom, the Buddha and his followers originally wandered throughout the year and never settled in one place. However, after a few years of this, they adopted the practice of settling in one place for the duration of the rainy season, a period of several months. Having a community of monks nearby was seen as auspicious by the laity, and it was not long before wealthy patrons built shelters where the monks could stay during this time. Eventually, these shelters developed into monasteries, which came to be inhabited throughout the entire year. Historical records indicate that in most countries, the monastic community became a settled, permanent institution, although the tradition of wandering monks still continues in places. Historical records also indicate that there have been—and continue to be—serious and often contentious debates about the appropriate rigor of monastic practices. The different interpretations of the Buddha's teaching on the rules for monastic communities are a continuing source of the many variations found among diverse monastic communities today.

Much as in Christianity, monasteries support themselves in different ways: some receive subsidies from the state, some own land that they lease for farming, some loan money at interest, and some make their money through tourism and pilgrims. Many monasteries also have rich traditions of education and are famous for the monks' many years of rigorous study, which includes memorizing lengthy texts and mandatory engagement in sophisticated doctrinal debate. This is particularly true of the monasteries in Tibet.

Buddhism also recognizes various orders of nuns, but their history is a bit more controversial. The story is told that shortly before the Buddha passed into final *nirvana*, one of his disciples, Ananda, asked him how a monk should relate to women. "Do not look at them," the Buddha replied. But if we see one? "Do not speak to them," the Buddha replied. But if a woman speaks to us? "Maintain mindfulness and self-control," the Buddha replied.[23]

However, in spite of the Buddha's seeming unwillingness to grant an order of nuns, it is said that he relented after his stepmother, Mahaprajapati, requested that the Buddha allow her and some

of her companions to become his followers. When
he refused, they shaved their heads, put on monk's
robes, and followed him anyway. Finally, Ananda
took pity on them and pleaded their case before
the Buddha. It took several different requests, but
the Buddha finally relented, allowing such an
order to be created. It should be noted here that it
is debated whether the Buddha himself instituted
the additional set of rules that ensure the subor-
dination of nuns to monks; some argue that these
were a later introduction, and that the additional
rules established by the Buddha himself—such as
not allowing them to walk in the forest by themselves—were for the nuns' protection. The order of
nuns has died out in several countries, but it still
survives in Korea, Vietnam, and China, where it is
particularly strong.

The relationship between monasteries and the
laity is extremely important for both parties. The
laity provides material support to the monks in
the form of food, money, and so forth; in return,
the monks convey merit upon the laity for their
support. Often this is just a general exchange,
but sometimes it is a more specific transaction in
which laypeople will give a donation in exchange
for a monk reciting a specific sutra. In essence,
monks do what laypeople cannot do—that is,
maintain a high level of purity by keeping an
elaborate set of vows. This practice causes the
monastery in general, and the monks themselves
in particular, to generate excess merit, which laypeople can receive by making offerings. Through
these offerings, the laity generate merit for a better rebirth for themselves in the future. It is for
this reason that monks are called "fields of merit";

by cultivating the monks, one receives a harvest of merit.

Again, as in Christianity, there are specific guidelines for monastic behavior. The rules of the Sangha, called the *Vinaya*, developed gradually and over time, often in response to a particular question or situation. It is said that there were no rules for monks during the first years of the Buddha's teaching, since the Buddha himself predicted that all his early disciples were destined for *nirvana* and therefore had gone beyond the point of needing rules for right behavior. All Buddhists, once they have taken refuge in the Three Jewels, take five vows: not to kill any living being, not to steal, not to engage in exploitive or harmful sexual activity (sometimes this is interpreted as celibacy, sometimes not), not to engage in speech that is false or harmful, and not to drink intoxicants. These vows are the most important, but in addition to these, there are many more vows a monk or nun takes upon ordination—in some of the Theravada traditions, there are over two hundred. These vows cover almost every aspect of personal and public behavior.

Four infractions warrant expulsion from the order: murder, sexual intercourse, stealing, and lying—particularly about the state of one's spiritual development. These correspond to the five vows listed above, with one exception: consuming alcohol is judged to be an offense one must confess, but it does not require expulsion from the order. In some monastic communities, monks have kept the practice of gathering twice a month to recite the monastic rules and make confession to the assembled members of the Sangha. All minor infractions require confession and also may entail a temporary loss of rights, some kind of penance, or a penalty of some kind.

In addition, one other sort of vows must be mentioned, the bodhisattva vows, which typically are taken by both monastics and by laypeople practicing within a school of Mahayana Buddhism. While the actual wording of the vows varies from school to school, the most important of the bodhisattva vows is the vow to achieve Buddhahood for the sake of all sentient beings. This creates an interesting point of tension between what we might call the "traditional" monastic vows and the bodhisattva vows, which occurs around the specific rules regarding infractions. While traditional monastic vows call for one to avoid specific nonvirtuous behaviors at all costs, bodhisattva vows actually make it an infraction for a bodhisattva not to be willing to commit a nonvirtuous act—such as stealing, lying, killing, or sexual misconduct—out of compassion for another. Thus, in the various Mahayana schools of Buddhism, many stories illustrate the compassion of bodhisattvas who committed nonvirtuous acts for the sake of others, such as the monk who accepted the sexual advances of a woman who threatened to commit suicide if he did not. Such an act is said to shorten one's path to enlightenment dramatically.

As discussed in this chapter, Buddhism is a religion in which soteriological goals are realized through specific practices that are believed to facilitate awakening. Keeping all this in mind, in the following chapter I return to a discussion of Christianity, suggesting new ways of understanding both the doctrine of salvation and the life such an understanding might engender for a Christian. In this way, I will demonstrate how an engagement with Buddhism has the potential to positively transform one's own beliefs and the practices of one's own faith.

5

Rethinking Salvation

Paul Griffiths writes that "soteriological methods are always linked with soteriological goals: what you do to get saved depends closely on what it is you think you need to get saved from."[1] Thus, it should be quite clear that it is impossible to simply import Buddhist practices and beliefs uncritically into a Christian context. Christians and Buddhists do not share all of the same soteriological goals, and thus the lives of faith they lead are not the same either. However, that does not mean that Christians have nothing to learn from Buddhists, or that Christians cannot experience a transformation in their own practices and beliefs through an engagement with Buddhism. In this final chapter, we turn our attention back to the Christian doctrine of salvation and reexamine it with new eyes, keeping in mind the discussions of the previous two chapters.

I would like to suggest three positive challenges to a traditional Christian understanding of salvation that Buddhist thought and practice raise. The first is the demand to relinquish an absolute claim to autonomy, in which Christians see their salvation primarily, or even exclusively, in terms of their own individual lives without taking into consideration the lives of others who interact with them and shape them on a daily basis. The second follows from the first; it is the demand to recognize humanity's fundamental interdependent existence and to see salvation as a culmination of these relationships: the collection and transformation of them rather than their abolition or dissolution. In short, an engagement with Buddhism impresses upon Christians the deeply communal nature of humanity and, consequently, the fundamentally communal nature of salvation as well.

The third and final challenge relates to the "when" of salvation, and the need for Christians to both appropriate and live out of a "salvation now" paradigm. Included in this analysis is a brief discussion of some interesting possibilities regarding the doctrine of universal salvation. I hope to show how all three of these challenges lead Christians to a deepened appreciation and understanding of salvation, and also to new insights into what it might mean to live in light of this new understanding: as in Buddhism, belief and praxis go together.

Relinquishing the Claim to Autonomy

Traditionally, a current of thinking exists in Christian theology, particularly in Protestant theology, that emphasizes the salvation of the individual without much consideration for her participation in the larger community. A classic example of this can be seen in the theology of John Calvin, specifically in his notion of election. While there is an element of the communal in Calvin's doctrine of election—he notes that God has chosen Israel in particular to be God's people—the heavily individualistic, discrete character of his doctrine cannot be avoided. Simply put, Calvin argues that, from the beginning of time, God has predestined some individuals for election while others God has given over to damnation. Calvin writes: "By predestination we mean the eternal decree of God, by which he determined with himself whatever he wished to happen with regard to every man [sic]. All are not created on equal terms, but some are preordained to eternal life, others to eternal damnation; and accordingly, as each has been created for one or other of these ends, we say that he has been predestinated to life or to death."[2]

While it is true that Calvin looks to an individual's calling and participation in the church as a confirmation of one's election, he never suggests that such participation might play a role in salvation, or that any human relationships come into play or are included in God's divine will for creation. Instead, Calvin, following Augustine here, argues that all creation is deserving of damnation, and so if God remits the punishment of even one individual, that is more than creation deserves. Thus, we are left with a picture of salvation in which some are plucked out and rescued from the mass destruction that awaits everyone else. God sees and judges each of us as individuals, and it is difficult to see where the relational aspect of humanity receives any consideration.

This is only one example, but this exclusive emphasis on the salvation of individuals reflects a commonly held belief that expresses itself in both positive and negative ramifications. The positive ramification of this idea is the confidence that God knows me by name and has entered into an intimate, personal "I-thou" relationship with me. Here, I have the assurance that no matter what else is going on in my life, no matter who I am alienated from or how alone I feel, I can take refuge in my relationship with God, trusting that God does not judge me the way the world judges me. However, the negative ramification of this idea is manifested in the fear people often express regarding the salvation or, more explicitly, the damnation of friends and loved ones outside the church. There is a concern that God relates to individuals exclusively on a one-to-one relationship and bases the decision for salvation or damnation solely on an individual's personal actions or beliefs. This excludes the possibility that interpersonal relationships might play a role in a person's final end and puts a great deal of pressure on the person individually.

Thus, even while I recognize the value of affirming God's relationship with each one of us particularly rather than generally, this exclusive focus on the individual aspect of Christian salvation has some very negative consequences. Specifically, I question whether, consciously or unconsciously, the belief that God acts to deliver us as discrete individuals encourages us to think of one another as competitors, either for God's favor or for a privileged place in the kingdom. Recall the story of James and John (Matt. 20:20-21), whose mother requested a seat for them at either side of Jesus. As can be imagined, the other disciples did not take this very well, and the very idea caused division among them. Even today, over two thousand years later, Jesus' disciples still compete for God's favor; and envy and jealousy still cause division within and without the church walls.

Rita Nakashima Brock and Susan Brooks Thistle-thwaite, in their powerful study of the culture of prostitution, note that "no human being is a human being without relationships, no matter how ambiguous. No person ever outgrows the need to know other living beings. This relational nature, in all its difficulty, is an inescapable fact of human existence. . . . But the United States, with its exaggerated notions of individualism and personal success, has done much to deny this relationality."[3] I agree with them on this point. To a marked degree in American society, we are encouraged to compete with one another for almost everything of value—wealth, job opportunities, physical prowess, social status, education. This includes the belief that we must be better than our neighbors in order to be the best; many advertising dollars are spent to persuade us that this one particular car/perfume/vacation/exercise program will make us the envy of our neighbors and give us the recognition we covet. This is nothing more than a secular longing for salvation, and it implies that true salvation must be competed for and won, or, at the very least, earned.

Ted Peters writes of this phenomenon eloquently in his book on sin. Peters maps out seven steps on the way to what he calls "radical evil." The first step he describes is "anxiety." Anxiety, he writes, is at its core a fear of loss. It arises out of a sense of insecurity, a concern over "a diminishment of who we are"—that is, a concern over our vulnerability, our weakness, and, in the end, our mortality.[4] In fact, Peters argues that the fear of death is at the heart of our anxiety, and this fear drives us to attempt to shore up our own existence by stealing the existence of others. We attempt to fortify our lives by plundering the lives of others, and that means primarily weakening them by taking their power. This action takes many forms, with varying degrees of severity: spreading malicious rumors about others, sabotaging their work, having affairs with their spouses, ridiculing them in public, raping them, killing them. When it is either "you or me" and our very lives are at stake, nothing can be ruled out.

What does this have to do with salvation? Plenty, I would argue. All too often, we play this same tragic game with ourselves as we contemplate our salvation. Often, we are secretly uneasy about our lack of power regarding our salvation. While it can be a source of great joy and relief that God grants us grace and forgiveness even though we do not deserve it, it can be a source of anxiety, too. It goes contrary to everything we are told in society—that is, that we all get what we deserve (it is poor people's fault that they are poor), and that we must earn what we want (there is no such thing as a free lunch).

Therefore, subtly or not so subtly, we go about trying to earn our salvation. This will give us assurance, we think; this will quell our fears of powerlessness. So we do good works, not out of love but out of fear. We go to church, not out of a sense of thankfulness but out of obligation. We keep a tally in our head of our behavior and measure ourselves against others to make sure they are not doing more than we are. Am I doing enough volunteer work? Am I tithing enough each week? How many Scripture passages have I memorized? Am I praying each night before I go to bed? Perhaps I think that if I can be better than the next person, God will choose me over her, and then I can be more confident in my salvation. Or, maybe I look around and think that if God chooses someone so lax and undeserving as him, God must also choose me, because I am so much better. There is an underlying competition in this attempt to earn salvation that stems directly from our anxiety about our powerlessness.

However, it is clear from Scripture that such attempts to earn our salvation are futile. We do not earn our salvation; it is a free gift from God. But even though at some level most of us know this, when we think of ourselves exclusively as discrete and independent individuals, we tend to think that our actions can gain or lose us favor with God. So we try to make ourselves look good—or at least better than our neighbors—and then we feel justified in claiming the rewards we are sure we've earned. Perhaps this is also one reason why people insist that God must judge and punish those we name as evildoers—murderers, rapists, terrorists. The danger is that if God actually forgives the worst of the worst, the lowest of the low, then all of our efforts to justify ourselves clearly are in vain, and the whole system of good and evil that we use to solidify our position in society and before God is nullified. This is an unhealthy and insidious way of thinking that causes division between us at the very point at which we should all be in solidarity—joy over the gift of our salvation in Jesus Christ. Does someone else really have to be damned in order to ensure that I be saved? Does hell have to exist in order to ensure that there is a heaven? This suggests a point at which engagement with

Buddhism might well provide a helpful way for Christians to look more deeply at the need to incorporate a notion of relationality into their core identity as well as their relationship with God.

In the face of all this individual competitiveness and resentment, it is worth asking what it would be like to envision ourselves as empty. How does a Buddhist idea of emptiness, which states that all living beings are empty of autonomous, independent being, change the way in which we relate to ourselves and to others? Several possibilities suggest themselves. First and foremost, seeing ourselves as empty recalls Paul's exhortation to Christians to live in Jesus Christ. In baptism, Christians die to the old life of sin and death and are reborn into the life and resurrection of Christ. In spite of this however, again and again we put on our old, worn clothes and leave our new robes in the closet. We know intellectually that we have been united to Christ, but we do not live out of that union because it is too risky—the realization of this transformation requires us to let go of our own selfish pursuits and live in the world as servants, transparent to the will of God. So, instead of seeing ourselves with new eyes, with the eyes of emptiness, and seeking our true existence in relationship with God and others, we cling to our old lives of independence and self-determination. We see ourselves as "full"—full of potential, full of strength, and full of freedom. To walk the path of emptiness puts all those crutches out of reach and forces us to see the lie they tell us: power, independence, and freedom promise something they cannot deliver—security. Security is the goal of the self, and it can never be attained; trust is the life of emptiness, and it is the only way to live before God.

Second, the concept of emptiness reminds us that we are to seek not after our own will but after the will of God. It calls us to a life of trust, a life of letting go, a life of openness to the grace of God. Being empty enables us to keep our hearts focused on Christ rather than on our own immediate wants and desires. For Christians, being empty means giving up one's own attempts at self-justification and allowing God's love and grace to flow through us unobstructed. Being empty means ceasing all grasping and clinging to individual glories, to self-promotion, to material rewards. Being empty means being transparent to God's purpose for our lives and allowing our relationship with God to define us, rather than seeking desperately to define ourselves.

Jesus himself modeled such a life of emptiness.[5] It is clear from the four Gospel accounts that Jesus acted with a wholly transparent understanding of selfhood. By that, I mean that he was fully open to the will of his Father, and in all things he submitted himself to the Divine. Perhaps the most obvious example of this is his prayer in the Garden of Gethsemane, where he lamented desperately that the cup of tribulation might pass from his lips—but only if this was God's will. "Yet not what I want, but what you want," says Jesus in Matthew 26:39.

If anyone was empty of clinging to his own self and jealously guarding his own ego, it was Jesus. Jesus did not seek fame for himself; nor did he try to preserve his life in the face of imminent death. He did not cling to wealth, to power, or to fame. Indeed, in the story of the devil's temptation of

Jesus in the wilderness, Jesus rejected everything that people tend to cling to in order to further their own sense of security and selfhood. He resisted food, even though he was famished. He rejected kingdoms and authority, even though they rightfully belonged to him. And, most interestingly, he refused to deliberately test God, refusing, I believe, to make such an aggressive, self-serving demand of God, even though he was God's most beloved Son. Jesus was empty of all instincts of self-preservation and self-aggrandizement, and sought his own fulfillment exclusively in the fulfillment of his Father's will and in the discipleship of his apostles. Thus, it seems to me that one way to understand the whole of Jesus' ministry is to see it as the work of a man who lived his life as though it were empty of independent existence.

A Buddhist understanding of emptiness, then, calls us out of the protective shells we have built for ourselves, out of our private fortresses, out of our independent and insular existence. Fundamentally, emptiness calls us into relationship, into true communion with God and with others. Emptiness frees us from the need for self-justification, from the need for competition and victory, and allows us to live in mutual dependence and harmony. Emptiness gives us room for others and gives us room for God. By not having to be concerned with our own salvation and self-preservation at every moment, we can turn outward and engage with others as true persons rather than as objects to overcome or conquer. We can focus on God without worrying about hiding our secrets or putting forth our accomplishments. We can listen to others without having to do all the talking. We can walk together without always having to lead. Finally, then, in seeing ourselves as empty, we see ourselves as we were created to be—interdependent and fundamentally relational. This concept of inherent relationality is the next idea in which Buddhism offers a helpful challenge to a Christian doctrine of salvation.

Recognizing Our Interdependent Existence

To review briefly, in Buddhism the doctrine of dependent origination, *pratityasamutpada*, points to the reality that human beings—and, in fact, everything in existence—do not first and foremost exist autonomously as themselves, only subsequently forming relationships with others. Rather, we come into being out of the network of those relationships and have no separable identity apart from them. Jay Garfield explains it this way: "There is no fixed boundary between the existence of a seed, the tree to which it gives rise, a piece of wood from that tree, and a table fashioned therefrom or between the existence of an intact table, a broken table, wooden table parts, ashes, earth, the nutrients for a seed, that seed, the sapling to which it gives rise, and another tree."[6]

Certainly, the notion of an interdependent existence is not new to Christian theology. In fact, it is quite old and is rooted in traditional discussions of the Trinity. Catherine LaCugna describes the connection between the intratrinitarian life of God and the relational life of human beings at some length in her book *God for Us*. Emphasizing the theology of the Cappadocian fathers in particular, although not to the exclusion of the Latin tradition, she notes the importance of the concept of relationship for understanding ontological claims about being—both God's being and our being. For both, "the meaning of to-be is to-be-a-person-in-communion."[7] For this reason, she emphasizes that "*Trinitarian life is also our life.* . . . The doctrine of the Trinity is not ultimately a teaching about 'God' but a teaching about God's life with us and our life with each other. It is the life of communion and indwelling, God in us, we in God, all of us in each other."[8] From this relational notion of the Trinity, we get a relational notion of human existence as well. In fact, LaCugna pushes the concept of relationship further. Not only is God fundamentally in relationship, and not only are human beings fundamentally in relationship, but indeed the entire cosmos is relational at its very core. The conclusion she draws then? "The Self can be a Self only in relation to other selves."[9] The problem, it seems, is not in Christian theology per se but in the Christian life—that is, putting the theory into practice.

That this is a particular problem in American society has not gone unnoticed. The authors of the book *The Good Society* challenge the traditional American view that places a premium on individual independence and casts suspicion on our communal institutions. Many Americans worry that institutions will take away their individual freedoms, the authors argue, while not realizing the degree to which the freedoms and independence they cherish are constructed and supported by the very institutions they malign. The authors then press the need for Americans to realize the degree to which we are all dependent upon one another and the institutions that we create together, which in turn help create us. They write:

> We are not self-created atoms manipulating or being manipulated by objective institutions. We form institutions and they form us every time we engage in a conversation that matters, and certainly every time we act as a parent or child, student or teacher, citizen or official, in each case calling on models and metaphors for the rightness and wrongness of action. Institutions are not only constraining but also enabling. *They are the substantial forms through which we understand our own identity and the identity of others as we seek cooperatively to achieve a decent society.*[10]

Although couched in political terms, the point here for us is the differing consequences that follow from different ways of conceiving of human existence. Such conceptions have ramifications in all aspects of our lives.

Without the recognition that our lives are deeply and inextricably bound together, we cannot help but view others as competitors rather than cocreators, as challengers to be vanquished rather than allies to be supported and befriended. The fact of our interdependent nature demands that we realize that in harming others we harm ourselves. There are many examples I could give to describe this reality: all members of a society suffer the effects of unemployment, even those who still have their jobs; all members of a society suffer when public education is underfunded, even those who are no longer in school. However, perhaps the best image that exemplifies this comes from Scripture: the image of the one body with many members.

In 1 Corinthians 12, Paul develops the analogy of the body of Christ. His purpose in making the analogy is to emphasize that although there are different gifts that the Spirit gives to different people, those differences are not more important than the fundamental unity of faith that holds them together. So Paul argues that just as the body is necessarily made up of different parts with different functions, such as the eye, the tongue, and the hand, for example, so also is the body of Christ necessarily made up of members who have different functions, such as healing, preaching, and teaching. The differences are necessary to form a body, Paul says, but they never supersede our common identity, our shared existence in Christ.

I would like to suggest that this image can be interpreted another way as well. It seems to me that this image also points to the need we have for genuine identification with others; the realization that if one member is injured then all members feel the effects. In other words, we must recognize that the health of the hand affects the functioning of the eye and vice versa. In verse 21, Paul writes: "The eye cannot say to the hand, 'I have no need of you,' nor again the head to the feet, 'I have no need of you.'" So too are we all mutually dependent on the health of one another, even though we often live as though we were completely independent. We like to think that each person has full control of his or her own well-being; and we pretend that we have responsibility only for ourselves, and that everyone else can and should just take care of himself or herself. This, however, is a patent falsehood.

We read this in verse 26: "If one member suffers, all suffer together with it; if one member is honored, all rejoice together with it." Even though Christians hear these words often enough in church, too often we do not take them seriously. We interpret them metaphorically and assume they are meant to stay within the church walls and are not to be retained after Sunday service is over. However, if we were to take Buddhism's deeply relational understanding of human nature seriously, we would come away with a more radical, more profound, and more literal interpretation of these words. If we were to follow a Buddhist interpretation of these words, we would feel hunger pangs in our own stomach when we saw someone begging on the street, rather than turn a blind eye. That is, we would feel the sufferings of another as though they were our own, rather than distance ourselves from them by insulating ourselves with our individuality.

In the same way, according to the Buddhist view of interdependence, we would rejoice with the person who got the job for which we also had applied, just as though we ourselves had been hired. We would applaud the play of the visiting team, even when they beat us. We would celebrate the wonderful opportunity of another, just as though we ourselves had that door opened to us. Ironically, I think celebrating someone else's success is sometimes even harder to do than having sympathy for someone else's misfortune. It is difficult for us to accept with grace the good fortune of others, because we are always thinking first and foremost of ourselves. So, when something good happens to someone we know, often our first thought is not

"What does that mean for her?" but, rather, "How does that affect me?" As I noted above, this excessively competitive view of human existence can easily destroy us, as we allow ourselves to be consumed by resentment and envy, not remembering that what is genuinely good for one is genuinely good for all. Buddhism's view of interdependent existence challenges us to broaden our vision to incorporate the whole body of the universe into our very selves, rather than focusing simply on our own particular member of that body, our own particular skin.

Incidentally, Christians have an excellent model for this type of behavior in the life and ministry of Jesus Christ. Jesus had a very different vision for what it means to be in relationship. Jesus sought out in particular those who were considered outcasts: the unclean, the marginalized, the ones off the social radar, such as lepers, prostitutes, and tax collectors. Over and over again, Jesus rebuked the disciples when they wanted to send people away, and he risked the condemnation of the ministers and scribes in order to acknowledge someone who reached out to him. In direct contrast to the attitude of those around him, Jesus responded to those in need as though they had a claim on him—that is, as though they were in relationship with him. He ate with tax collectors and sinners, he stood up on behalf of an adulteress, and he accepted little children onto his lap. Jesus pushed the boundaries of what it means to be in relationship far beyond what the society at the time had ever considered. In fact, Jesus gave his life in order not to exclude anyone from a life-giving relationship with God.

Salvation Now

The final challenge Buddhism presents to a Christian understanding of salvation can best be seen through the lens of the tension between the "now" and the "not yet" character of Christian salvation. As we discussed in chapter 2, one of the main characteristics of Christian soteriology is its "now/ not yet" character, which is often described using the concept of prolepsis, the present anticipation of a future reality. This concept of prolepsis allows Christians to live in the present time, with all its imperfection, while still holding on to a vision of future consummation and redemption, seen in the life, death, and resurrection of Jesus Christ. In Christ, Christians believe, we have a vision of what will be true for all of us in the "not yet," even though we must still live, fragmented, in the "now." It is this vision of the "foretaste of the feast to come" that brings the future experience of salvation into the present. Prolepsis is the name for this collapsing of time between the now and the not yet.

In Christian life, salvation is realized now insofar as we recognize that our reconciliation to God has been effected, that God's forgiveness of our sins already has been granted in the death and resurrection of Jesus Christ. We are here and now children of God. We are here and now united in the body of Christ. We have already died to our old lives of sin and death and are risen in the life of Jesus. We do not have to wait for our salvation; it has been granted us already. At the same time, however, we can look around and realize that our relationship to God is still broken, marred by the sinfulness that continues to characterize our lives. We hope for something better, for the complete restoration of creation and the day when all our tears will be wiped away. In the meantime, as Paul says, we still do that which we do not want to do and still turn from God every day. Clearly, our salvation, while already given, has not been perfected. There is an aspect of our salvation that remains an unrealized promise and compels us to look to the future for its fulfillment.

Under the best of circumstances, this tension is difficult to maintain. One of the most common ways the balance gets skewed is that Christians tend to neglect the present aspect of their salvation, looking away from the now toward the not yet. It is tempting for Christians to overlook the fact that, to some degree, we have been given heaven on earth already—at the very least, a taste of heaven—and thus we are called to live our lives here as though the kingdom had already come. This is not to say that we can and should entirely collapse the distinction between God's kingdom and our own context—only God can bring the kingdom in its fullness. However, we can accept the salvation we have already been given and live out of it now instead of passively waiting for what is to come. Seeing the kingdom here among us is something akin to seeing the face of Jesus in the faces of our neighbors. It means recognizing that we do not have to wait for a new day; it has already dawned. It means realizing that we live in the presence of God moment to moment, even though that presence is sometimes veiled. It means accepting that Jesus has come into the world and left us with his Spirit to bind us to God and to one another. It means confessing that our new lives have already begun and that we live now as children of God.

How might Buddhism assist Christians in this new orientation to the world? In chapter 4, I noted that Nagarjuna's interpretation of the Buddhist doctrines of *samsara* and *nirvana* led him to the conclusion they are not in radical opposition: enlightenment is not somewhere else, something different from the suffering world in which we live today. Instead, it is seen and experienced right in the middle of the rhythm of one's daily life, and indeed, even more radically, it is identical with one's daily life. I believe this insight can help Christians focus our attention on our salvation here and now more constructively, in that it calls us to a more rigorous ethic, a more loving anthropology, and a more vigilant ecological awareness.

To explicate this more thoroughly, let me begin with the metaphor "the kingdom of God." When Christians pray the second petition in the Lord's Prayer, they are praying for the longed-for coming of God's kingdom—that is, for the end of all sin, death, and evil; the end of what Martin Luther calls "the devil's kingdom." In this sense, it is clearly a prayer for the future, a prayer for the realization of the "not yet." However, if that is all it is, if it is left as simply a passive hope for the future, the metaphor has been distorted and misunderstood; and unfortunately, far too often that is exactly what happens. Thus, I argue, given this traditional Christian interpretation of God's coming kingdom, a third place where Buddhism can influence a Christian concept of soteriology is the way in which a Buddhist understanding of the equivalence of *nirvana* and *samsara* challenges Christians to see the kingdom as present right now, rather than projecting all of our visions of salvation onto the not yet; and to live as though the kingdom were here right now rather than waiting for it to come sometime in the far off "not yet."

What this challenge demands is no less than a radical change of mind-set, a change in one's attitude toward the world in its entirety. Motivated by this Buddhist identification of *nirvana* with *samsara*, Christians are able to envision a new motivation for ethical action in the world. Instead of working to model God's coming kingdom, what if the church were to work to protect and celebrate God's present kingdom? Instead of focusing on the ways in which the present world is not the kingdom (admittedly, there are many reasons it is not), thereby emphasizing the discontinuity between the two, what if the church were to focus on the continuities between world and kingdom, and, indeed, seek to stabilize and develop those continuities—not attempting to bring about the coming of God's kingdom but rather in humble recognition of the many ways in which the kingdom is already among us?

I recognize that this sounds heretical, a Pelagian attempt to force God's hand, perhaps. This, however, is not what I am suggesting at all. No one but God can bring out God's kingdom; there is no loophole, no catch, and I am not insinuating otherwise. What I am offering instead is a new model of experiencing salvation in the world, a new way of envisioning our relationship both to the kingdom and to the cosmos. This model does not do away with the tension between the now and the not yet; nor does it try to avoid it. Rather, it shifts the focus from God's coming kingdom to God's present kingdom and makes the reality in which we live now our starting point. The task, then, is not to model what is to come but to tend and transform what is now, recognizing that it is our sacred vocation to maintain and foster the present reality of God's kingdom, particularly in light of all the forces of evil that conspire against us. To act as though God's kingdom were already in our midst would be to view the here and now as something to be celebrated, protected, and tended with loving care.

To illustrate what I am proposing here, let us think for a moment about the difference between people who live in a house they rent versus those who live in a house they own. It is common knowledge that most people who are renting a house do not care for it the way they would if it were their own. They do not make as many repairs, they do not concern themselves as much with the beauty of the garden or the yard, and they do not see themselves as deeply invested in the house. Often, they do not take time to get to know the neighbors next door or to participate in block parties or community activities. This is not surprising, because in many cases, renters are temporary lodgers, looking to the day when they will move on.

Contrast this attitude with that of home owners. Those who own a home typically have made an important investment and commitment to the property. They have purchased only after long deliberation and only when they have found something that they love. And once they move in, they care for it because they know they are responsible for it, and they take both pride and pleasure in its

upkeep. Further, they often take the time to cultivate relationships with those around them, to get
to know and become friends with those people with
whom they share a fence or a sidewalk. This, too,
is not surprising, given that everyone on the block
has a common interest in protecting and preserving their shared space. This means watching the
houses of neighbors when they are gone. It means
joining forces to keep cars from speeding down
the street. It means looking out for the children of
others as though they were your own. Owning a
house means focusing on the right here and right
now, not assuming the present is a throwaway, a
disposable means to some other end.

In her book *Life Abundant*, Sallie McFague uses
a similar analogy to advocate for what she calls
"ecological economics." In her words, we need to
see ourselves as "members of nature's household"
rather than as consumers of nature's wealth.[11] In
the first model, a sense of communal responsibility and interdependence is presupposed, as each
individual sees herself as part of a larger whole
on which she depends and which depends on her
for health and sustainability. In the second model,
an estrangement between creation and individuals
is presupposed, a competition in which the latter
uses the former as means to their own selfish ends.
The model of household members emphasizes
responsibility, care, and "sustainability," the same
points I want to highlight in my model of humans
as home owners rather than tenants.

Now I want to extend this model to the way
we think of our present context—not only to the
physical buildings in which we dwell but also to
the people who form our communities and the

landscapes that define our living spaces. Are we merely passing through these spaces, consuming their wealth, to use McFague's image, without taking any responsibility of ownership? Is our community, our society, our nation, our planet a temporary lodging place, a means to an end, or is it a home, an end in itself?

When it comes to a new understanding of salvation, shaped by Buddhism, these questions are of critical importance. As a way of suggesting a fruitful answer, I argue that Nagarjuna's claim that "nirvana is samsara and samsara is nirvana" can be interpreted helpfully by Christians as "the kingdom is the cosmos, and the cosmos is the kingdom." This formula suggests that instead of the view in which the kingdom of God appears light-years away, we should adopt a more immediate view of the kingdom, a view in which God is nearer to us than we are to ourselves, in which God's kingdom is just around the corner, close enough for us to feel. As Ted Peters describes it, in this view we occasionally experience God "slowing down," as it were, and allowing us to experience God's presence in a particular, miraculous way, so that we can see in advance the wholeness of the kingdom.[12] This vision of the kingdom's nearness—indeed, the immediate inbreaking of salvation now—gives us the impetus we need to make this world the best possible world that it can be for all of us, recognizing that this earth is our home, the people of the planet are our neighbors, and God is here in our midst right now. It is true that the kingdom is yet to come, but perhaps it is not so far off as we often assume. Perhaps it is only as far away as the next moment.

I want to briefly suggest two more important ramifications of this model. First, when we envision ourselves as living in God's kingdom now, we are called to see both ourselves and others as redeemed and loved now, as we are. We need not fear our failings and weaknesses or worry that our misdeeds will keep us from God's presence. To put it another way, in our very weaknesses, in our very sinfulness, we are also experiencing the kingdom of God. We can be gentle with ourselves and with our defects and sins, for in this too God is bringing about God's kingdom. We live with God already, and thus we do not need to feel that we must work ourselves into God's favor. God has already favored us with salvation and mercy. To experience God's kingdom now is to experience ourselves as saved, and that in itself is a great grace and gift of faith.

Second, this model calls us to take seriously Paul Tillich's conviction that the sacred and the secular are found only intertwined and cannot be opposed. Tillich writes that "the holy and the secular belong to each other."[13] We cannot ever fully separate them nor set them in opposition. When we assume ourselves able to distinguish confidently between the holy and the profane, we immediately fall into sin, as we begin pointing fingers and drawing lines to keep out the undesirables. In doing so, of course, we are always in the sacred circle, and it is others who are out. We are the embodiment of good; they are the embodiment of evil. We attempt to reserve the kingdom for ourselves, and we presume to know how to separate the wheat from the tares. However, this is all a facade, a lie. The truth is that the holy does not destroy the profane, the sacred does not obliterate the secular, and the kingdom does not destroy the cosmos but instead redeems and transforms it. The kingdom is not opposed to creation but exists in, over, and through it. The new Jerusalem that is promised in Revelation is still recognizable as Jerusalem, after all.

Nagarjuna's idea that *nirvana* is *samsara* and *samsara* is *nirvana* reminds us to be wary of black-and-white distinctions between what is of God and what is of this world. God's choice to enter into the world means that nothing in creation is out of the reach of God's presence. In Jesus Christ, God has chosen to exist among evil, and thus the glimpses we have of the kingdom now are intermingled with images of the world; and similarly, the images we have of the world are accompanied by impressions of the kingdom. They do not cancel each other out. Our lives here and now are not separated from the kingdom but, rather, are enhanced by and infused with it. We live in the world, and we live in the kingdom simultaneously. Both are our home.

The Possibility of Universal Salvation

There is one last idea that these three Buddhist ideas of emptiness, dependent origination, and *nirvana/samsara* suggest to me, although I admit it is perhaps a bit more speculative than the conclusions reached above. However, as it deals directly with the Christian understanding of salvation, it is worth considering. Basically, I want to explore a theory of universal salvation that is grounded in our inherent relationality, recognizing that in light of our interdependence, God does not relate exclusively to individuals through Jesus Christ but, in the incarnation, has actually put Godself into the heart of the relational cosmos, thereby reaching out to and encompassing every living being through our relationships to one another and to God.

This relational understanding of salvation is true to both the interdependent existence of creation and the divine will that all be saved. What's more, it also does not require that individuals be thought of as "anonymous Christians" in order to be included under the all-encompassing umbrella of God's love; this relational understanding of salvation does not demand the affirmation that all people of all religions end up in heaven—whatever that might mean or look like. As I noted at the very beginning of this chapter, different religions teach different religious ends, different doctrines of salvation, if you will, and those differences must be respected.[14] A doctrine of universal salvation that is based on the inherent emptiness and relationality of all life in the cosmos and that recognizes the presence of salvation here and now demands from the Christian only a belief in God's all-embracing love and a realization that our very humanity is constituted out of a dynamic, all-encompassing network of living, pulsating relationships. God can safely be trusted with the rest.

The strength of such an idea is its recognition of the fact that God has willingly enmeshed Godself in creation and thus is bound up inextricably in the relationships of all people, not just Christians. Logically, then, we must concede that God is absent from no human relationship and is present to all of humanity equally, relationally. This is one way in which we experience the gift of God's grace on a daily basis. God's grace, given in our very existence as human beings, enables us to live in right relationships with one another, and this means that we do not have to come into explicit, conscious contact with Jesus in order to experience God's grace, even though Christians trace the ontological source of that grace to Jesus Christ. What this means is that it is not our responsibility to put ourselves in relationship with God for salvation to occur—God has already done that for us—and therefore, if we understand salvation to be the participation in the life of God, salvation has been given already to everyone.

I recognize that there will be objections to this theory. First, some would argue that such an overarching "meta-narrative" of salvation does not do enough justice to the radical difference between religious traditions. This is a point well taken. My only defense is that Christians already have been given a meta-narrative in the life, death, and resurrection of Jesus Christ, and it is, in some ways, incumbent upon us to be as inclusive with it as we can, pushing ourselves to see universal meaning in this life-giving story. But at the same time, as a Christian, I certainly must keep in mind the limits of my own perspective, recognizing that it is distinct from the perspective of those adhering to different religious traditions; they may well see things differently than I.

Second, not everyone would agree that "participation in the life of God" is the best way to define salvation. If salvation is defined as the forgiveness of sins, for example, then recognition of and belief in Jesus Christ are required; otherwise, one cannot experience the divine power to forgive and heal. This is also true if salvation is defined as confessing Jesus Christ as my personal Lord and Savior. However, I would argue that, first and foremost in the Christian tradition, salvation is the gift of restored relationship with God. It is the gift of reconciliation and grace, and it is the assurance of God's presence with us, God's attention and God's providence. In this view, then, what salvation primarily promises is new life in God and participation in the coming kingdom. Given what we have learned about human existence from our study of Buddhism, these promises make sense only in a relational context. If I do not even exist as a discrete individual, how can I understand my participation in the kingdom as anything but a fulfillment and transformation of all the relationships that constitute my existence now? If my own life is already inherently relational, how can my new life in God be anything less, if it is still to have continuity with what I know and experience as my life now?

Perhaps this is too much to believe in, too much to assert as dogma, but, at the very least, can we not, as Hans urs von Balthasar writes, at least *hope* that all are saved?[15] Can we not hope that if there is, in fact, a hell beyond the hell that many people experience right here and now, it is empty? Isn't it enough for hell to stand as a powerful, vivid image for the experience of utter godforsakenness, which, since Jesus Christ himself descended into hell and filled it with his presence, has been destroyed forever? For Christians, it seems that anything less is uncharitable at best and deeply sinful at worst, given what Christians confess about salvation. Christians believe that in Jesus Christ, we have the promise that the relationships that are broken and hurtful now will be restored in the future and will become life giving. We have the promise that our estrangement from God and from others will not last forever but will be overcome by our unity in God. We have the promise that those relationships we cannot see and cannot feel will one day become present to us, and that we will one day experience ourselves as whole, as members of one body. While God's participation in created relationality does not always seem to change things now—there is still suffering and death, alienation and isolation—we have the promise that change is coming, and will come, in the form of a final beatitude and peace that will course through all of our relationships like blood in our veins, circulating God's love and grace throughout the entire creation unobstructed. How can we possibly, in good conscience, not wish this for everyone?

Theology for the Future

I hope to have demonstrated that Christians can gain several important insights from Buddhist thought that can help us rethink some of our central soteriological claims. Further, I hope to have modeled one fruitful method of engaging in the task of interreligious dialogue, and to have shown how this type of interreligious inquiry never leaves one unaffected but, rather, always deepens one's own understanding both of oneself and of the other. True dialogue is always "effective," and its participants always end up standing in a new place, seeing themselves, and others, with new eyes.

Finally, my hope is that this engagement between Christianity and Buddhism will be influential on several fronts. First, the time is right for a reexamination of the traditional assumptions of Christian soteriology, given our current context of increased cultural and religious sensitivity. Christians are more aware now than ever of the vast differences that separate people of distinct nations and cultures, yet many still long for a unified vision of wholeness that does justice to our common humanity and shared existence in the world. Here I seek to honor the former, by recognizing and analyzing the dissimilar truth claims asserted in Buddhist and Christian worldviews, while still remaining faithful to the latter, through a demonstrated commitment to the universal scope of God's salvific action in Jesus Christ.

Further, I see practical, pastoral ramifications in this analysis as well, as questions of one's own salvation and the salvation of others are some of the most poignantly felt of all Christian theological inquiries. The love we have for one another in relationship leads us to want the best for our loved ones, and sometimes this hope is in conflict with traditional church teachings. There continues to be a lack of critical tools with which people of faith can sort out the difficult question of how to reconcile the conflicting views of salvation in different religious traditions. Thus, I hope this work might encourage critical, creative thinking in Christians who wrestle with the issues of their own salvation and the salvation of others.

This leads to my final conclusion. I hope that it is clear from the preceding analysis that inter-religious dialogue is not a task peripheral to systematic theology. Rather, it stands at its core and is an indispensable component of expressing the Christian faith with relevance and coherence in a diverse, multifaceted world. Theology that takes no notice of the truth claims of other religions betrays the very church it is supposed to serve, and abandons the very people it was supposed to nourish and support. Theology that ignores the difficult questions raised in conversation with people of other religious traditions relegates itself to irrelevance and obscurity, and will, in the end, cause people to go elsewhere seeking faithful answers to the questions in their hearts and on their lips. Christians should not fear engaging with other religious traditions, if only because we trust God is with us and because we know how much we have to learn, not only about others but, perhaps even more importantly, about ourselves. God is not done with us yet, and we must use wisely the gift of time that we have. Every conversation is a discovery; every insight, a grace.

> Great Nature has another thing to do
> to you and me; so take the lively air;
> and, lovely, learn by going where to go.[16]

Notes

Preface

1. John Bowker, ed., *The Oxford Dictionary of World Religions* (Oxford: Oxford University Press, 1997), 844.

2. S. Mark Heim, *Salvations* (Maryknoll, N.Y.: Orbis, 1997), 144.

Chapter 1: The Task at Hand

1. Hans-Georg Gadamer, *Truth and Method*, 2nd ed., trans. Joel Weinsheimer and Donald G. Marshall (New York: Continuum, 1994), 260 (author's italics).

2. Ibid., 484.

3. Ibid., 290.

4. Ibid., 462.

5. Ibid., 309.

6. Ibid., 310.

7. Ibid., 299.

8. Ibid., 97.

9. Ibid., 384.

Chapter 2: A Christian View of Salvation

1. María Pilar Aquino, "Theological Method in U.S. Latino/a Theology," in *From the Heart of Our People*, ed. Orlando O. Espín and Miguel H. Díaz (Maryknoll, N.Y.: Orbis, 1999).

2. For an excellent treatment of this idea, see Barbara Rossing, *The Rapture Exposed: The Message of Hope in the Book of Revelation* (Boulder, Colo.: Westview, 2004).

3. Ivone Gebara, *Longing for Running Water* (Minneapolis: Fortress Press, 1999), 90.

4. Ibid., 89.

5. I want to note here an interesting question raised by the recognition of this power of autochthony: whether this very local, individual-specific phenomenon can be expanded to encompass the world as a whole. Or, more specifically, is there a way in which deep connection to the mountains of Colorado might be enlarged to encompass the coast of Australia and the arid plains of the Gobi Desert? In other words, is it possible to capitalize our feelings of autochthony to get to a cosmic sense of belonging and responsibility?

6. James H. Cone, *A Black Theology of Liberation* (Mary-knoll, N.Y.: Orbis, 1998), 139.

7. Ibid., 141.

8. James H. Cone, "Strange Fruit: The Cross and the Lynching Tree," *Harvard Divinity Bulletin* 35, no. 1 (2007): 51.

9. One good introductory resource that discusses a wide variety of atonement themes is David Brondos's *Salvation and the Cross* (Minneapolis: Fortress Press, 2007).

10. These are often referred to as "theories" of atonement, but I am intentionally avoiding that language. To Western ears, the language of "theory" suggests something that eventually will be proven or disproven, with the addition of more information. By contrast, motifs of atonement function more metaphorically to suggest constructive, meaningful ways of articulating the powerful, saving truth of Jesus' life, death, and resurrection. They are not contradictory; nor are they hypothetical. Instead, they stand together as a testimony to the wide variety of ways in which Christians have experienced the reality of God's redeeming work in Jesus Christ.

11. Gustaf Aulén, *Christus Victor*, trans. A. G. Hebert (New York: Collier, 1986), 4.

12. Ibid., 5.

13. Ibid., 6.

14. *Sermons on the Gospel of John, Chapters 1–4, Luther's Works*, vol. 22, ed. Jaroslav Pelikan (St. Louis: Concordia, 1957), 24.

15. Dennis Weaver, *The Nonviolent Atonement* (Grand Rapids: Eerdmans, 2001), 11.

16. Ibid., 210.

17. Ibid., 20.

18. Ibid., 21.

19. Ibid., 37.

20. Ibid., 74.

21. Ibid., 79.

22. "Declaration on the Relation of the Church to Non-Christian Religions," in *Vatican Council II* (Collegeville, Ind.: Liturgical Press, 1987), 739.

23. "Dogmatic Constitution on the Church," in *Vatican Council II*, 367.

24. Ibid., 367

Chapter 3: Introducing Buddhism

1. This is the vow one takes to declare oneself a Buddhist. It states one's commitment to the truth of the Buddha, the truth of the Buddhist community, and the truth of the Buddha's teaching. As Donald Lopez writes: "In the medical metaphor of which Buddhists are so fond, the Buddha is the doctor, the dharma is the medicine, and the sangha are the nurses. It is the Buddha who finds the path to liberation and shows it to others. The dharma is the path itself, and the sangha are one's companions who offer assistance along the way." Donald S. Lopez Jr., ed., *Asian Religions in Practice* (Princeton, N.J.: Princeton University Press, 1999), 64.

2. Donald S. Lopez Jr., *The Story of Buddhism* (San Francisco: HarperCollins, 2001), 12.

3. Donald W. Mitchell, *Buddhism* (Oxford: Oxford University Press, 2002), 9.

4. Lopez, *The Story of Buddhism*, 19.

5. *Buddhist Birth-Stories,* trans. Rhys Davids (Calcutta: Srishti Publishers, 1998), 150–51.

6. John Strong, *The Experience of Buddhism* (Belmont, Calif.: Wadsworth, 1995), 15.

7. Richard Robinson and Willard Johnson, *The Buddhist Religion* (Belmont, Calif.: Wadsworth, 1997), 14.

8. Notice that this episode suggests that even the Hindu gods were still subject to the karmic cycle of rebirth, and thus even they needed the Buddha to show them the path of liberation. This was one way in which Buddhism subordinated Hindu gods to the Buddha and asserted the superiority of its teachings.

9. Lopez, *The Story of Buddhism*, 56.

10. Mitchell, *Buddhism*, 36.

11. Lopez, *The Story of Buddhism,* 43.

12. See Melford Spiro, *Buddhism and Society: A Great Tradition and Its Burmese Vicissitudes,* 2nd ed. (Berkeley: University of California Press, 1982).

13. Lopez, *The Story of Buddhism,* 47.

14. Richard K. Payne, "The Anti-Ritual Stance of Buddhist Modernism and Its Implication for the Relations between Buddhism and Psychotherapy" (paper presented at the conference "Deep Listening, Deep Hearing: Buddhism and Psychotherapy East and West," University of Oregon, Eugene, July 29–August 1, 2006).

15. Lopez, *The Story of Buddhism,* 47.

16. *The Lotus Sutra,* trans. Burton Watson (New York: Columbia University Press, 1993), xix.

Chapter 4: A Buddhist Understanding of *Nirvana*

1. I follow the account as recorded by David Ross Komito in his book *Nāgārjuna's Seventy Stanzas: A Buddhist Psychology of Emptiness* (Ithaca, N.Y.: Snow Lion, 1987), 17–18.

2. Nāgārjuna, *Nāgārjuna: A Translation of His Mulamadhyamakakarika with an Introductory Essay,* trans. Kenneth Inada (Tokyo: Hokuseido Press, 1970), 3.

3. C. W. Huntington Jr. with Geshe Namgyal Wangchen, *The Emptiness of Emptiness* (Honolulu: University of Hawaii Press, 1989), 29.

4. Roger Jackson, "For Whom Emptiness Prevails: An Analysis of the Religious Implications of Nāgārjuna's *Vigrahavyavartani,*" *Religious Studies* 21, no. 3 (September 1985): 14.

5. Chr. Lindtner, *Nagarjuniana: Studies in the Writings and Philosophy of Nāgārjuna* (Copenhagen: Akademisk Forlag, 1982), 41.

6. Ibid., 97.

7. Nāgārjuna, *The Fundamental Wisdom of the Middle Way,* trans. Jay Garfield (New York: Oxford University Press, 1995), 331.

8. Ibid., 332.

9. Daigan and Alicia Matsunaga, *The Buddhist Concept of Hell* (New York: Philosophical Library, 1972), 60.

10. Bruce Matthews, *Craving and Salvation* (Ontario: Wilfrid Laurier University Press, 1983), 19.

11. This relates to the larger distinction between *nibbanic* and *kammatic* Buddhism, which was mentioned in chapter 3. Again, for a more in-depth discussion of this distinction, see Melford E. Spiro, *Buddhism and Society* (New York: Harper and Row, 1970).

12. Donald S. Lopez Jr., ed. *Asian Religions in Practice* (Princeton, N.J.: Princeton University Press, 1999), 67.

13. Thich Nhat Hanh, *The Miracle of Mindfulness,* rev. ed., trans. Mobi Ho (Boston: Beacon, 1987), 11.

14. Paul J. Griffiths, "Indian Buddhist Meditation," in *Buddhist Spirituality,* ed. Takeuchi Yoshinori (New York: Crossroad, 1993), 34.

15. Ibid., 46.

16. From *The Saundarananda of Asvaghosa,* cited in John Strong, *The Experience of Buddhism* (Belmont, Calif.: Wadsworth, 1995), 121.

17. Donald W. Mitchell, *Buddhism* (Oxford: Oxford University Press, 2002), 1164–65.

18. For more detail and beautiful color pictures, see Barry Bryant, *The Wheel of Time Sand Mandala* (San Francisco: HarperSanFrancisco, 1992).

19. For an example of engaged Buddhist analysis, see Rita M. Gross, *Soaring and Settling* (New York: Continuum, 1998).

20. As quoted in Mitchell, *Buddhism,* 271.

21. This story is told in Donald S. Lopez, *The Story of Buddhism* (San Francisco: HarperSanFrancisco, 2001), 122–23.

22. Richard K. Payne, "Mantra, Dhāraī, Daimoku and Nenbutsu: Four Instances of the Ritual. Use of Language," paper presented at the conference on "Language and Discourse in the Transformation of Medieval Japanese Buddhism," at Green Gulch Zen Center, Marin, California, September, 2001.

23. Lopez, *The Story of Buddhism,* 157.

Chapter 5: Rethinking Salvation

1. Paul J. Griffiths, "Indian Buddhist Meditation," in *Buddhist Spirituality,* ed. Takeuchi Yoshinori (New York: Crossroad, 1993), 42.

2. John Calvin, *Institutes of the Christian Religion,* vol. 2, trans. Henry Beveridge (Grand Rapids: Eerdmans, 1975), 206.

3. Rita Nakashima Brock and Susan Brooks Thistlethwaite, *Casting Stones* (Minneapolis: Fortress Press, 1996), 287.

4. Ted Peters, *Sin* (Grand Rapids: Eerdmans, 1994), 34.

5. Those familiar with Buddhist/Christian dialogue will recognize this line of thinking. The Christian concept of kenosis, particularly as found in Philippians 2:5-11, has been related to the Buddhist doctrine of *sunyata* by a variety of scholars, most notably Masao Abe. See his essay and others in John Cobb and Christopher Ives, eds., *The Emptying God* (Maryknoll, N.Y.: Orbis, 1998).

6. Nagarjuna, *The Fundamental Wisdom of the Middle Way,* trans. Jay L. Garfield (New York: Oxford University Press, 1995), 199.

7. Catherine Mowry LaCugna, *God for Us* (San Francisco: HarperSanFrancisco, 1973), 250.

8. Ibid., 228 (italics in original).

9. Ibid., 256.

10. Robert N. Bellah et. al., *The Good Society* (New York: Vintage, 1992), 12 (my italics).

11. Sallie McFague, *Life Abundant* (Minneapolis: Fortress Press, 2001), 106.

12. Ted Peters, Systematic Theology lecture, Pacific Lutheran Theological Seminary, Berkeley, California, October 16, 2001.

13. Paul Tillich, *Systematic Theology*, vol. 3 (Chicago: University of Chicago Press, 1963), 248.

14. This begins another separate and interesting line of thinking, which unfortunately is beyond the scope of this paper. For provocative, insightful work on the idea of multiple religious ends, see S. Mark Heim's two books, *Salvations* (Maryknoll, N.Y.: Orbis, 1995), and *The Depth of the Riches* (Grand Rapids: Eerdmans, 2001).

15. Hans urs von Balthasar, *Dare We Hope "That All Men Be Saved"? With a Short Discourse on Hell* (Ft. Collins, Colo.: Ignatius, 1988).

16. Theodore Roethke, "The Waking," in *Americans' Favorite Poems*, ed. Robert Pinsky and Maggie Dietz (New York: Norton, 2000), 241.

Glossary

ahimsa: Literally, "non-harming." This doctrine teaches a reverence for all life and describes a practice of avoiding hurting or killing any living creature. It is a component of many Indian schools of thought, but it is of particular importance in Jainism and Buddhism. It is practiced with varying degrees of observance: from vegetarianism, for example, to going out of one's way to avoid harming even a spider or mosquito.

arhat: One who has attained the final stage of enlightenment through lifetimes of strenuous, devoted practice.

avatar: The name given in Hinduism for the manifestation on earth of a specific deity. It is comparable, but not identical to the Christian doctrine of incarnation.

bodhisattva: One who has taken a special vow to use the merits of one's practice through the course of many lifetimes in order to help all sentient beings attain awakening.

chakpur: The name for the metal tube used by Tibetan monks in the creation of sand mandalas. One is filled with colored sand, and then rubbed gently by another one to release the grains of sand onto the design.

Dharma: A general term that refers to the teachings of the Buddha.

dukkha: The Sanskrit term for suffering, it points to the general state of unhappiness and dis-ease that characterizes the way in which unawakened/unenlightened people experience their lives.

Eightfold Path: The means by which one is able to free oneself from the suffering of this world. It refers to eight elements (Right Understanding, Right Thoughts, Right Speech, Right Action, Right Livelihood, Right Effort, Right Mindfulnes, and Right Concentration) that are meant to be practiced together in order to facilitate the realization of enlightenment.

Four Noble Truths: The heart of the Buddha's first sermon and the core of his teaching.

karma: Many Buddhists hold that karma is the driving force behind the cycle of rebirth, which characterizes life for all sentient beings. According to karma theory, every action has a consequence–good actions generate good consequences, bad actions generate bad consequences–and these consequences will come to fruition in either this or a future life.

Mahayana: The name for the schools of Buddhism that developed as Buddhism began to move into East Asia, which adopted some significantly different practices and teachings regarding enlightenment.

mandala: An elaborate, colorful visual diagram that contains depictions of a particular Buddha or bodhisattva with a wide variety of symbols and images that are meant to further one's understanding of central Buddhist doctrines. Through the practice of visualization, one is able to enter into this sacred space and experience oneself as a part of it.

mantra: A specific phrase that functions as a powerful invocation, addressed to a specific Buddha or bodhisattva. It is repeated in order to deepen one's connection to that figure and actualize the qualities possessed by him or her.

mindfulness: In a general sense mindfulness refers to the sense of being present to the actuality of one's existence at all times.

moksha: Liberation from the cycle of death and rebirth.

mudra: The name for the particular hand gestures that typically accompanies a specific mantra or particular visualization practice. The gesture is meant to encourage the embodiment of one's spiritual practice.

Nagarjuna: A key interpreter of the Buddha's teachings for the Mahayana Buddhist schools; born in India sometime in the first centuries CE.

nirvana: The experience of enlightenment, when one sees the truth of existence and is freed from delusion and suffering.

pitaka: Literally, "basket." This is the name given to the different collections of Buddhist texts. There are three *pitikas*, which together constitute the Buddhist canon.

pratityasamutpada: Often translated as "dependent origination," it points to the reality that all beings exist in relationship to other beings, and these relationships are constitutive of their being.

samsara: The way one typically experiences the world, characterized by desire and suffering.

Sangha: The name for the Buddhist monastic community.

soteriology: Literally, "words about salvation"; hence, the term refers to religious teachings and doctrines about salvation; the study of what it means to be saved.

stupa: A monument in which relics of the Buddha or another Buddhist saint are housed and venerated. A *stupa* is typically dome-shaped, but can be more elaborate.

sunyata: The doctrine of emptiness, which states that all beings are "empty" of independent, eternal, autonomous substance and existence.

sutra: Literally the word means "thread" in Sanskrit. It refers to teachings (or sermons) of the Buddha.

Theravada: This term is often used to designate the schools of Buddhism that constitute the earliest form of Buddhism, practiced primarily in South Asia.

upaya: This doctrine of "skillful means" points to the willingness of the Buddha and other bodhisattvas to use any means necessary in order to teach human beings the truth about reality, thereby leading them to enlightenment.

Vajrayana: This form of Buddhism, practiced primarily in Tibet, teaches a swift path to enlightenment; the possibility of enlightenment in one's current incarnation, rather than waiting for a more favorable rebirth.

Vinaya: The name for the collection of the rules for Buddhist monastic communities.

Further Reading

To Learn More about Buddhism

Conze, Edward. *A Short History of Buddhism*. Oxford: One-world, 1993.

Gross, Rita. *Soaring and Settling*. New York: Continuum, 1998.

Hanh, Thich Nhat. *The Diamond That Cuts through Illusion*. Berkeley, Calif.: Parallax, 1992.

_____ . *The Miracle of Mindfulness*. Boston: Beacon, 1987.

Lopez, Donald. S., Jr. *Prisoners of Shangri-La*. Chicago: University of Chicago Press, 1998.

_____. *The Story of Buddhism*. San Francisco: HarperSanFrancisco, 2001.

Mitchell, Donald W. *Buddhism: Introducing the Buddhist Experience*. New York: Oxford University Press, 2002.

Nagarjuna. Translated by Jay Garfield. *The Fundamental Wisdom of the Middle Way*. New York: Oxford, 1995.

Price, A. F. and Wong Mou-lam, translators. *The Diamond Sutra and the Sutra of Hui-Neng*. Boston: Shambhala, 1990.

Robinson, Richard and Willard Johnson. *The Buddhist Religion*. Belmont, Calif.: Wadsworth, 1997.

Strong, John S. *The Experience of Buddhism*. Belmont, Calif.: Wadsworth, 1995.

Watson, Burton, translator. *The Lotus Sutra*. New York: Columbia University Press, 1993.

Williams, Paul. *Mahayana Buddhism*. London: Routledge, 1989.

To Learn More about Buddhist/Christian Dialogue

Cobb, John. *Beyond Dialogue*. Philadelphia: Fortress Press, 1982.

Cobb, John, and Christopher Ives, editors. *The Emptying God*. Maryknoll, N.Y.: Orbis, 1990.

Fredericks, James. *Buddhists and Christians: through Comparative Theology to Solidarity*. Maryknoll, N.Y.: Orbis, 2004.

Hanh, Thich Nhat. *Living Buddha, Living Christ*. New York: Riverhead, 1995.

Heim, S. Mark. *Salvations*. Maryknoll, N.Y.: Orbis, 1997.

Ingram, Paul, and Frederick Streng, editors. *Buddhist-Christian Dialogue: Mutual Renewal and Transformation.* Honolulu: University of Hawaii Press, 1986.

King, Sallie, and Paul Ingram, editors. *The Sound of Liberating Truth.* Surrey, U.K.: Curzon, 1999.

Luz, Ulrich, and Axel Michaels. *Encountering Jesus and Buddha.* Minneapolis: Fortress Press, 2006.

Nakasone, Ronald, editor. *The Transforming Spiritual Landscape: Buddhist-Christian Encounters.* Fremont, Calif.: Dharma Cloud, 2005.

Pieris, Aloysius, S.J. *Fire and Water.* Maryknoll, N.Y.: Orbis, 1996.